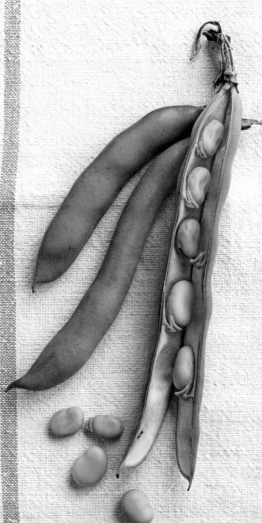

Beans,
Peas
& everything
in between

Beans, Peas

& everything in between

More than 60 delicious, nutritious recipes
for legumes from around the globe

Vicky Jones

photography by **William Reavell**

RYLAND PETERS & SMALL
LONDON • NEW YORK

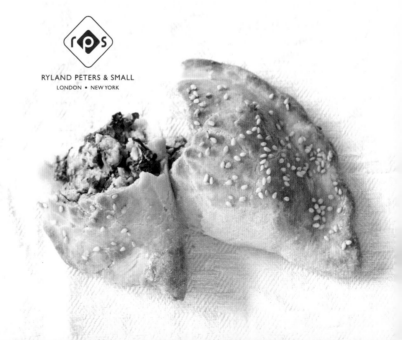

Designer *Barbara Zúñiga*
Commissioning Editor *Nathan Joyce*
Head of Production *Patricia Harrington*
Art Director *Leslie Harrington*
Editorial Director *Julia Charles*
Publisher *Cindy Richards*
Indexer *Hilary Bird*

Prop Stylist *Linda Berlin*
Food Stylist *Rosie Reynolds*
Cover Illustrator *Lucia Catellani*

Originally published in 2015
as *'Out of the Pod'*.
This revised edition published in 2022
by Ryland Peters & Small
20–21 Jockey's Fields
London WC1R 4BW
and
341 E 116th St
New York
NY 10029

www.rylandpeters.com

Text © Vicky Jones 2015, 2022
Design and photographs © Ryland Peters & Small
2015, 2022
Illustration © Lucia Catellani 2022

ISBN: 978-1-78879-444-2

10 9 8 7 6 5 4 3 2 1

A CIP record for this book is available from the
British Library.
US Library of Congress Cataloging-in-Publication data
has been applied for.

Printed and bound in China

Notes
• All references to fava beans in these recipes refer to
split dried fava (dried fava beans). However, as the
US English term 'fava' also refers to fresh broad beans,
not dried ones, this may lead to confusion. The only
recipe in the book containing fresh broad beans is
Broad Bean Soup for Springtime (see page 37).
Furthermore, fava beans should not be confused with
Greek fava, which is made from dried split peas.

• Both British (Metric) and American (Imperial plus
US cups) are included in these recipes for your
convenience, however it is important to work with
one set of measurements and not alternate between
the two within a recipe.

• All spoon measurements are level, unless otherwise
specified.

• All herbs used in these recipes are fresh, unless
otherwise specified.

• All eggs are medium (UK) or large (US), unless
specified as large, in which case US extra-large should
be used.

• When a recipe calls for the grated zest of citrus fruit,
buy unwaxed fruit and wash well before using. If you
can only find treated fruit, scrub well in warm soapy
water before using.

• Ovens should be preheated to the specified
temperatures. We recommend using an oven
thermometer. If using a fan-assisted oven, adjust
temperatures according to the manufacturer's
instructions.

Contents

introduction 6

1 SOUPS 19

2 STREET FOOD 43

3 SALADS 65

4 MAIN DISHES 81

5 VEGETARIAN MAIN DISHES 107

6 SIDE DISHES & DIPS 125

7 DESSERTS 143

suppliers & stockists 154

index 156

acknowledgements 160

Introduction

There's nothing more delicious than food with a good story and this applies particularly to the collection of recipes in this book, all of which are based on dried beans, chickpeas and lentils. Legumes have been staple foods from the very beginnings of agriculture and in many parts of the world, they remain so. Soups and stews based on dried beans, lentils, chickpeas and peas are still the ultimate comfort foods the world over, the recipes often unchanged over millennia.

The extraordinary versatility of these humble ingredients is brought out in a rich variety of recipes inspired by the cooking traditions of countries where legumes are still eaten on a regular basis, from Latin America to India, from Spain to Serbia. Just as each of the dishes can be traced back to its culinary roots, so can the ingredients. Nothing can be more exciting than tracing the origins of a particular bean or pea, or sampling a dish in the very place where it evolved thousands of years ago – a path of discovery which can provide endless pleasure.

About half of the recipes are vegetarian, while the rest use meat or fish, often quite frugally and more as flavouring for the beans, chickpeas or lentils which are the backbone of the dish. Many can be prepared quickly if time is short, while others are left to simmer slowly for many hours, as they were in the past.

The world of legumes

This book is about a remarkable family of food plants, the **legumes**. They all produce pods with neat little rows of seeds inside, which humans have harvested for food since the Stone Age. These seeds – beans, peas and lentils – are highly nutritious and satisfying and have traditionally formed a vital part of the diet of many cultures throughout the world, being high in protein and carbohydrates, as well as minerals and vitamins.

The other great feature of the Fabaceae family (the botanical name for all leguminous plants) is that their edible seeds can be preserved by the simple process of drying, so can provide food throughout the year. When dried, legume seeds are are known to many as **pulses**, an older word which came from the Latin puls, meaning 'thick soup'.

Until 1492, pulses lived in two separate worlds, the Old World and the New World. **Lentils**, **chickpeas**, **broad/fava beans** and **peas** were first domesticated in the Fertile Crescent region of what is now eastern Turkey, Iraq and Syria. It is here that the earliest archeological evidence of the cultivation of legumes has been found, dating from about 7,000 BC. To this day, these are the most popular pulses in Middle Eastern cookery, used in an astonishing number of different ways from creamy dips to aromatic soups and stews.

Meanwhile, across the ocean in Mexico, their close relatives, the *Phaseolus* beans, were being gathered from the wild and later cultivated. It was not until Spanish explorers discovered America in 1492 that beans were brought back to Europe and later spread around the world. So it was at this time that the ancestors of **borlotti**, **cannellini** and **butter/lima beans** met their cousins the chickpeas, lentils, broad/fava beans and peas for the first time.

New World legumes

Varieties of *Phaseolus vulgaris*, the botanical name for the common bean, come in many shapes, sizes and colours. **Black turtle beans,** so called because of their dark, shiny shells, are oval in shape and jet black, with a dense, meaty texture and a mushroomy flavour.

In cooking, their striking appearance seems to invite many dramatic colour combinations, with red (bell) peppers or tomatoes, with bright green avocados and fresh coriander/cilantro, with yellow pumpkin and corn, or as a complete contrast, with white rice. Their culinary home is firmly in Latin America, and that is the inspiration for most of the black bean recipes in the book.

Red beans also belong primarily to Latin America and the Caribbean, their native lands, where they are at home with the hot spicy flavours of the tropics. Red beans and rice is a combination which is utterly emblematic of the Creole cuisine of Louisiana. Other red bean enthusiasts include the people of northern India and the inhabitants of Georgia, where red beans are combined with plum sauce, or walnuts, or used to fill pies.

Red beans have a meatiness that is hard to ignore. Maybe it's because they look rather like tiny kidneys, or possibly because they stay in one piece more readily than many other beans and therefore lend themselves to long, slow cooking – either way, they really are the archetypal poor man's meat.

Pinto (meaning 'painted'), **scritto** (meaning 'written'), **borlotto**, **Tongue of Fire**, **Caribbean rosecoco**, **cranberry** and **bird's egg** are all colourful mottled beans with wonderfully descriptive names. When freshly shelled they are quite the prettiest of pulses, some splashed with magenta or maroon on a pale green or cream background, others speckled pink on cream. Bicolour varieties exist, beautifully marked with a symmetrical, yin-yang pattern in maroon or black and white.

When dried, mottled beans turn a rather sad shade of beige, but they have a lovely nutty flavour and a pleasant mealy texture reminiscent of chestnuts. They form the basis of many rustic Italian soups and stews and are an everyday staple in Mexico, where they're mashed as refried beans.

With their distinctive pale green colour and delicate flavour, **flageolet beans** have always been associated with elegant cooking, compared to their less refined cousins. They were never grown to feed starving peasants, but were initially cultivated on private estates to supply the tables of the

aristocracy of Europe. Relative newcomers on the bean scene, French flageolets were originally bred from a mutant dwarf bean by Gabriel Chevrier, a gardener who lived in the village of Brétigny-sur-Orge, just south of Paris, in the 19th century.

Whereas all beans start off green, most take on other colours as they mature, or simply fade to a creamy-white, but M. Chevrier noticed that the mutant beans in his garden remained green much longer than normal and so he set about breeding from them to preserve this pale green colour.

White beans are the backbone of many iconic dishes in Europe and North America, from *cassoulet* to *fabada* to Boston baked beans. As with most of the ingredients that came from the New World, Spain was the first country to cultivate beans, soon to be followed by the Italians and the French, and it is in the kitchens of these countries that white beans still hold sway.

Known botanically as *Phaseolus lunatus,* the large white beans called **butter/lima beans** are a bit of a mystery. Confusingly, some varieties of the **runner bean**, *Phaseolus coccineus*, are also classified as butter beans. Another variety of Phaseolus coccineus is the Italian **fagiolo di Spagna**, which grows in temperate climates such as our own. When buying canned butter/lima beans, look out for the ones which are packed in Italy, as they are fagioli di Spagna and have a superior taste and texture.

Old World legumes

Chickpeas/garbanzos *(Cicer arietinum)*
Chickpeas are much loved in the Middle East, where they were first cultivated more than 8,000 years ago. One the mainstays of Arab cooking, they are also widely used in countries around the shores of the Mediterranean, from Sicily to Catalonia via North Africa, where the influence of Muslim Arab culture has made its mark on local cuisine.

The Arabic word for chickpea is *houmus*, a word which has also come to signify the ubiquitous dip of chickpeas, sesame and lemon, which is now available ready-made from virtually every supermarket and grocery store.

The vetch-like plant has feathery leaves, grows to an average of 60 cm/2 ft. in height and bears numerous papery pods with a fuzzy surface, each containing just one or two seeds.

Chickpeas can be classified into two main types: *kabuli* (from Kabul), which are larger and white or cream in colour, and *desi* (from the countryside), which are much smaller and range in colour from light tan to black. Kabuli chickpeas are generally grown in temperate regions, and consumed whole, whilst the desi type require a semi-arid tropical climate and are mainly grown in the Indian subcontinent, where they are skinned and split and known as *chana dal*, or ground into besan/gram flour, used mainly to make batter for pakoras or for thickening curry sauces.

Chickpea/gram flour is also used in Italy and France to make delicious pancakes and fritters, called *farinata*, *cecina* or *socca*, depending on where you happen to be.

Chickpeas can even be eaten fresh, and when young and tender they taste and look rather similar to garden peas, brilliant green in colour. Nibbled raw, they have a refreshing taste and a pleasantly crunchy texture.

Lentils *(Lens culinaris)*
One of the most ancient of foods, lentils have been a staple part of the Mediterranean diet since the Stone Age. Before the advent of farming, they were gathered from the wild, along with the seeds from various grasses, and these were the first crops early man chose to cultivate. It seems nothing short of a miracle that the potential of the lentil as food was ever identified, so tiny and insignificant are they in their mini-pods, each containing only one or two seeds.

Lentils were an everyday food amongst the ancient Egyptians, Greeks and Romans, although they were often associated with poverty. Pliny the Elder thought that they promoted an even temper and the Roman cookery book author *Apicius* provides several appetizing recipes using lentils which would stand up well today. The Egyptians even placed lentils in tombs as an offering to the dead.

Today we take both **brown lentils** and **Puy lentils** for granted, while the precious, slate-blue **Castelluccio lentils** from a remote plateau in Umbria, or the tiny black '**Beluga**' lentils which look like caviar and hold their texture remarkably well, have taken their place in the rare ingredients department.

On a global scale, India is both the greatest producer and also consumer of lentils, eaten mainly in the form of dal. Lentils play a vital role in feeding the world, today more than ever. The plant is tolerant of different soil types, even those with low fertility, so it can be grown on marginal lands and has a vital part to play in the field of food security.

Peas *(Pisum sativum)*

Dried peas have been a staple food in European and Mediterranean countries since ancient times, reaching southern Sweden by the Iron Age. They are easy to grow and store, and are high in carbohydrate and protein, so it is easy to see why dried peas were such a vital part of the diet, both for animals and humans.

They were eaten by the ancient Greeks, the Romans and the Egyptians, either as soup or in a thicker form as a kind of porridge/oatmeal. But today, peas are the pulse of the north, more popular in Scandinavia and northern Europe than around the Mediterranean.

Every northern European country has its own split pea soup. England has the *London Particular*, a tasty soup enriched with ham or bacon, and named rather unfortunately after the dense 'pea-souper' industrial fogs that used to engulf large cities before the Clean Air Act of 1956. France has its *Potage Saint-Germain*, enriched with cream, and named after the market garden close to Paris which was once famous for its peas. Sweden has *artsoppa*, made with yellow split peas, pork and onions and traditionally served on Thursdays, while the Netherlands has *erwtensoep*, also known, rather less attractively, as *snert*, with green split peas, leek and celery amongst its ingredients. In Hungary, *sargaborso*

leves includes, as might be expected, lard and paprika, and Berlin is famous for its *gelbe erbensuppe* which usually contains yellow split peas, bacon and root vegetables.

Pea soup was one of the first convenience foods ever to come on the market, when *Erbswurst* – compressed pea soup tablets packed in a sausage-shaped roll – was manufactured on a vast scale to feed German troops during the Franco-Prussian War of 1870–71. It only ceased production recently.

Today, peas are still grown for drying on a large scale in Britain and North America. Marrowfat is a popular variety for its high yield, grown not only for mushy peas but for export to the Far East, where roasted dried peas are a popular bar snack. Crunchy wasabi-coated peas are now a snack of choice in many countries, often imported from China or Japan.

Broad/Fava Beans *(Vicia faba)*

The ancestral home of the broad/fava bean is the Middle East, where they were first cultivated well over 5,000 years ago, along with chickpeas and lentils. It is thought that the Romans brought them to Britain and found that they thrived in the cool, mild climate. Today, they are widely grown commercially in Britain, and enjoy increasing popularity when eaten fresh or frozen, but a large proportion are dried and exported, mostly to the Middle East and North Africa, especially Egypt, where they are treated with the respect they deserve and considered a vital part of the diet.

However, home-grown dried broad/fava beans have recently begun to appear in the shops in Britain, under the label Hodmedods. Imported dried broad/fava beans can also be found in Middle Eastern, Turkish or Greek food stores, or in some Italian delicatessens. They can be bought whole or skinned and split – these break down completely when cooked, and make beautifully smooth creamy dips and soups.

They are the basis of Egyptian falafel and *ful medames*, a garlicky dish of cooked and mashed fava beans served with hard-boiled/cooked eggs and lemon juice, which is eaten morning, noon and night; Sicilian *maccu*, a thick soup which has been a staple food since ancient times; *favata*, a hearty Sardinian stew of pork and beans with wild fennel; and *fave con cicoria*, a broad bean purée served alongside sautéed wild greens in Puglia.

Black-eyed Beans/Peas *(Vigna unguiculata)*

Although they look similar, black-eyed beans/peas have a completely different ancestry from the other beans on the dried food shelves of supermarkets and grocery stores across the world. Their motherland is tropical West Africa, where the vast majority are still consumed today. Very much a staple food, they are made into nourishing soups and stews such as *ewa*, savoury cakes like *moi moi*, or fritters and pancakes called *akara*. From Africa they spread to the shores of the Mediterranean and to Asia, reaching India about 1,500 BC. They were loved by the ancient Greeks and Romans, and until the discovery of the New World, were the only beans known in Europe apart from broad/fava beans.

Black-eyed beans/peas are popular taverna fare in modern Greece too, often cooked with garlic and juicy greens, or simply served with some fruity olive oil and a squeeze of lemon. They also found favour in Catalonia, where they are known as *mongets* or *fesolets*, and often found alongside grilled *botifarra*, the local pork sausage, or in salads with anchovies or salt cod.

But black-eyed beans/peas are most famous for the central part they play in the cuisine of the American Deep South, where they have become indelibly identified with soul food. Black-eyed beans/peas are prolific and grow in hot climates without much cultivation, water or care, so were eaten not only by enslaved Africans but by poor white colonists as well.

Mung Beans and Dal

It is scarcely credible in this age of globalization that some of India's most highly prized legumes are hardly known in Europe except by the Asian community. They have amongst the highest protein content of all pulses – about 25 per cent – and also enjoy the reputation of being the easiest to digest. On top of that they have a good flavour, so it's a real mystery why we don't appreciate or utilize them more.

Red lentils (*masoor dal*) have been widely available for many years, but other split pulses have remained largely unknown, which is our loss.

The word dal refers in India not just to the spicy, soupy mush we all know and love, but rather loosely to any dried split pulse. Masoor dal (red lentils) are actually the skinned and split version of green lentils, while **chana dal** is skinned and split chickpeas; **moong dal** is from green mung beans, toor dal is red gram, **urid dal** is black gram, and so on. All are quick to cook and very easy on the digestive system.

Moong dal, which could easily be mistaken for yellow lentils, cooks to a smooth purée in a very short time – about 20 minutes – and seasoned with spices and served with rice or Indian bread, makes a nutritious and tasty instant meal.

Urid dal is creamy white and can be ground into flour, which is extensively used in pappadoms and southern Indian preparations such as *idli* (steamed dumplings) and *dosas* (pancakes).

Soya Beans/Soybeans

Soya beans/soybeans contain more protein than any other pulse and have sustained populations in China, Japan and South-East Asia for centuries. However, to become fit for consumption, they must first be processed in some way. In the Far East they are fermented to make foods such as miso, tempeh and tofu, as well as soy sauce.

The beans are also rich in oil; this oil is, in fact, the world's most important source of cooking oil. For this reason they are usually classed as an oilseed rather than an edible pulse. They are widely used in processed industrial foods and as animal fodder, but are too indigestible to be used in domestic cooking.

Heritage Varieties

The relatively narrow range of pulses in shops are usually produced on a vast scale, but there are thousands of other varieties of beans, chickpeas and lentils which are grown in remote areas by gardeners on tiny plots of land, often organically. They can often be spotted in local markets, or flagged up as a speciality of the region in country areas of Spain, Italy and France as well as in the USA. Many are in danger of disappearing, as they are very labour-intensive to produce and are now regarded as Heirloom or Heritage varieties or protected by a Protected Geographical Indication (PGI) in an attempt to preserve them.

Some fetch what seem like exorbitant prices, but they are of such high quality that people are happy to pay the going rate. Tracking them down is like panning for gold, so snap them up if you get the chance. With their thin skins and buttery interiors, they need nothing more complicated than a splash of olive oil, some garlic and herbs as dressing to make them memorable. Many have their own annual festival to celebrate their existence (see pages 58–9.)

Goodies and Baddies

Goodies

Most people know the childhood rhyme 'Beans, beans, good for your heart...,' for its reference to the windy aspect of eating legumes, but the opening line has now also been shown to contain more than a grain of wisdom.

In 1960, John F. Kennedy said 'You can't tell me that anyone who uses beans instead of meat in the United States is well fed or adequately fed.' How times have changed. Health organizations all over the world over now recommend the regular consumption of pulses/legumes because studies have identified a number of benefits which are

especially significant at a time when diet-related disease is at an all-time high.

Significant amongst these benefits, apart from their protein content, are the high amounts of complex carbohydrates, including soluble and insoluble fibre. Soluble fibre is known for its beneficial effect on cholesterol, considered to be one of the main risk factors in heart disease, while insoluble fibre maintains a healthy digestive system and may reduce the risk of colon cancer. The complex carbohydrates are slowly digested, thus preventing blood sugar levels from rising too quickly, and this makes pulses/legumes especially useful in the control of diabetes. Chana dal (split chickpeas) is especially good in this way, as it has an exceptionally low glycaemic index, but all legumes are beneficial. Obesity, another major problem throughout most of the world, can also be controlled by including pulses/legumes as part of a balanced diet, as they are low in fat but fill the belly effectively.

Pulses/legumes are packed with nutrients, containing substantial amounts of vitamins and minerals in relatively few calories. They contain significant amounts of essential minerals such as calcium, iron, zinc, selenium and potassium and are also particularly rich in B vitamins, including folate, thiamin and niacin. Folate lowers homocysteine levels in the blood and so is thought to be protective against heart disease and stroke. Just one portion of beans, lentils or peas provides half of the daily requirement.

But it is probably for their high protein content that pulses/legumes are best known, which is why they are often dubbed the poor man's meat. Containing between 20–25 per cent protein, this figure is much increased when pulses/legumes are combined with grains, as they often are. Pulses/legumes account for 10 per cent of the total dietary protein consumed in the world and have about twice the protein content of most cereal grains, but it is only when pulses/legumes and grains are consumed together that a complete protein is obtained, as certain amino acids are missing in both. Luckily these just happen to be complementary, so by eating beans with rice, for example, a complete protein is obtained.

Most of the recipes in this book combine pulses/legumes with grains, or can be served alongside bread or rice to achieve the same end. This is a formula which has sustained populations since the beginning of time and almost every culture has its own version of it. Think of Tuscan bean and farro soup, houmous with pitta bread, Indian dal with chapatti, or good old beans on toast.

To sum up, here are 12 good reasons for eating pulses/legumes:

1   Versatility. Good in soups, stews, fritters, pancakes, pies or sweet pastries, there are a thousand ways to cook pulses/legumes
2   The ultimate comfort food the world over, and a potent symbol of peasant cookery
3   Their amazing capacity to absorb flavours of aromatics and seasonings
4   Stress-free, they can be prepared in advance and reheated, or kept warm. Often even better reheated the next day
5   They're economical
6   High protein content, especially when combined with grains, so ideal for vegetarians or to reduce meat consumption
7   Nutrient dense, abundant in B vitamins, especially folate, thiamin and niacin, and containing key minerals including iron, zinc, selenium and potassium
8   High fibre content lowers cholesterol and promotes a healthy digestive system
9   Satisfying and slowly absorbed, so especially good for weight control and stabilizing blood sugar levels; associated with a reduced risk of diabetes
10 Eco-friendly: easily stored at room temperature without the consumption of fossil fuels
11 Readily available from supermarkets, health food shops and market stalls
12 An important crop for sustainable agriculture; legumes have the capacity to use nitrogen from the atmosphere to enrich the protein content of both the plant and the seed and subsequently to fertilize the soil.

Baddies

Flatulence is a subject that people pretend they would rather not discuss, at the same time as delighting in the topic. Even in Chaucer's day the topic caused great amusement:

> 'This Nicholas anon leet fle a fart
> As greet as it had been a thonder-dent...'

Flatulence and beans are inextricably linked in people's minds. But although the problem can't be eliminated completely, there are various ways that it can be reduced to perfectly acceptable levels (for more details, see pages 15–17).

The cause of these offending gases is that, as well as containing a variety of beneficial ingredients, dried legumes also comprise certain compounds called oligosaccharides which human digestive enzymes are unable to cope with. They, therefore, leave the upper intestine unchanged and when they reach the lower gut are immediately devoured by hungry bacteria, giving off hydrogen, methane and carbon dioxide gases which are expelled by the body, causing embarrassment to the perpetrator and offence to those nearby.

This might be troublesome, but more serious is the fact that raw pulses/legumes also contain natural toxins, called lectins or haemagglutinins, which can cause severe gastrointestinal reactions including nausea, diarrhoea and vomiting. Undercooked red kidney beans are the main culprits of such nasty problems, but white beans can also be equally harmful, as sadly, I know to my cost.

The illness only arises if you eat uncooked or undercooked beans, when these lectins bind cells in the gastrointestinal tract, damaging the structure of red blood cells by causing them to clot together. However, recovery is usually rapid and spontaneous, taking place 3–4 hours after symptoms first present themselves.

The following table, provided from information accessed by the UK's Food Standards Agency (FSA), illustrates the different amounts of haemagglutinins found in various types of legume. The quantity of toxin present is expressed in haemagglutinating units or HAU per gram of beans. As a rough guideline, up to 400 HAU is considered to be a perfectly safe amount to consume.

Casting an eye at this chart, it is easy to see why mung beans, either whole or split and skinned (moong dal) can be ground to a paste after soaking and used to make quickly-cooked pancakes such as dosas without any ill effects. In a similar way, dried broad/fava beans are used to make falafel, which are only fried briefly in very hot fat. Ground soaked chickpeas are sometimes used to make falafel, and while they do contain more lectins than broad beans, are completely safe as long as they are properly cooked through.

By contrast, dried kidney beans, red or white, should always be boiled briskly in fresh water for 10 minutes after soaking and draining, then simmered until tender, to make them safe for eating, as they contain up to 1,000 times more of these toxins than mung or broad/fava beans. Eating just one or two raw beans can trigger symptoms, and a normal portion can make you extremely ill. It is also worth bearing in mind that undercooked beans may be more toxic than raw ones.

Butter/lima beans should also be treated with caution and should never be eaten raw, as they can contain different toxins which are cyanide precursors. Although modern breeding has all but eliminated these potentially harmful compounds, it is best to play safe and make sure that butter/lima beans are soaked and boiled for 10 minutes in an uncovered pot in order to release and destroy the toxins, before simmering gently until soft.

TYPE OF PULSE/LEGUME	RAW	FULLY COOKED
Red kidney beans	Up to 102,000 HAU	200-400 HAU
White kidney beans	Up to 70,000 HAU	200-400 HAU
Soy beans	800–30,000 HAU	n/a
Chickpeas/garbanzo beans	400 HAU	n/a
Black gram/whole urid beans	100 HAU	n/a
Whole mung beans	100 HAU	n/a
Broad/fava beans	90 HAU	n/a

Canned or dried?

One of the major preoccupations of our age is how to save time. We all seem to be busy, and want everything instantly, while at the same time supporting such organizations as the Slow Food movement, which promotes another way of thinking altogether.

With relation to beans and cooking, there is the dilemma of whether to open a can or soak dried beans or chickpeas and cook them the next day. It sounds so easy but somehow, it's even easier to forget to do it. Lentils, split peas, mung beans and dal do not generally need preliminary soaking and cook relatively quickly, so there's no problem there.

There's no doubt in my mind that dried beans and chickpeas, soaked and cooked from scratch are more appetising and easier to digest. Also, they are cheaper. But apart from the burden of having to plan ahead, dried beans can take 1 hour or more to cook, which adds to the cost and can put people off altogether. It's better, in this case, to open a can.

As long as the water is unsalted, nutrients are unaffected by the canning process, but the taste and texture can be substantially different from those cooked from scratch. It may be due to the high temperatures to which the beans are exposed during the preparation process, but both the flavour and texture are likely to suffer.

Canned beans and chickpeas vary enormously. Generally speaking, coloured and speckled beans seem to survive the process in better shape than white beans, which often turn to mush if even slightly overcooked, or worse still, can have tough skins which separate from the bean and make for unpleasant eating. They have tough skins because the manufacturers often select varieties such as North American navy/haricot beans expressly for their tough skins, which hold together during long cooking; however, the downside is that they do also tend to have a coarse, mealy texture and less flavour. These shortfalls can be overcome when the beans are sold in a strongly flavoured sauce, which masks the quality of the beans themselves, as in the case of baked beans.

Even different brands of canned beans in water can vary enormously. I first noticed this when I bought some butter/lima beans which had been canned in Italy, and the difference was astonishing. Not only did they have a wonderful creamy texture, but also their skins were thin yet intact – a far cry from the ones canned in the UK, which are by comparison tasteless and often have thick, tough skins.

Again, the variety of bean selected by the canning companies varies, too. Italian butter/lima beans are called *fagioli di Spagna*, whereas British and American processors favour lima beans for canned butter beans.

Bottled beans and chickpeas, often from Spain, are also of exceptionally high quality. They are quite hard to find, and relatively expensive, but again the difference is very noticeable.

Canned black, red and speckled beans, such as borlotti and pinto, are generally of a fairly consistent quality which is perfectly acceptable for most uses, as are canned chickpeas, although I have sometimes found these need additional cooking as they can be a bit bullet-like. They should all be drained of their liquid and rinsed before use, especially if the water is salted.

Buying and storing

The golden rule when buying pulses/legumes is to buy them from shops and grocery stores that have a rapid turnover and where the sell-by dates on the products are clearly visible. Packets that lurk dustily at the backs of shelves are likely to be past their prime and are best avoided. Market stalls are often a good source of dried beans and peas, but are often quite lax about labelling the produce with use-by dates.

By comparison with other foods, dried beans, peas, lentils and chickpeas have an incredibly long shelf life. But although they will remain edible for decades, they should really be consumed within a year, as after that they begin to harden and take longer and longer to cook.

They are best stored in airtight glass jars in a cool, dry place.

Soaking

All dried beans, whole peas and chickpeas should be soaked in water before cooking.

There are two reasons for this: first, it reduces the cooking time, and second, it removes some of the complex sugars or oligosaccharides contained in pulses/legumes that cause flatulence. Lentils, mung beans, split dried fava beans, black-eyed beans/peas and split peas do not need soaking, although they will cook more quickly if they have been pre-soaked.

The soaking water

The skins of dried pulses/legumes soften much more readily in soft (alkaline) water, while hard (acid) water will slow up the cooking process considerably. For this reason, many people recommend adding a little bicarbonate of/baking soda (about ¼ teaspoon per litre/quart) to the soaking water, especially if your tap/faucet water is hard. This has the effect of softening the skins quickly, reducing cooking times.

However, by adding bicarbonate of/baking soda, certain nutrients such as thiamin are thought to be lost into the soaking water and flavour can be adversely affected, so a choice has to be made.

When fully hydrated, dried pulses/legumes will have doubled in volume, so use a large enough container. The traditional method of soaking is to put the beans in a bowl with 3 times their volume of cold water and to leave them overnight or for at least 8 hours, before draining and cooking them in fresh water.

The quick soak method is to place the pulses/legumes in a saucepan with 3 times their volume of water, bring it to the boil, simmer for 2–3 minutes, then leave to soak for 1 hour or more in the same water before draining and cooking. In 1 hour, the beans absorb as much water as they do in 15 hours of soaking in cold water.

Large beans and chickpeas need a longer soaking time than small beans. If using the long soak traditional method, butter/lima beans and chickpeas should be soaked for 24 hours, changing the water several times.

Leave beans in the soaking water until they are fully hydrated, when the skins are completely smooth and not wrinkled.

Although split peas, lentils and black-eyed beans/peas do not need long soaking, they should be thoroughly rinsed until the water runs clear.

Cooking

Drain and rinse the beans, throwing away the soaking water, and put them in a saucepan. Pour in just enough fresh water to cover, but don't drown the beans, or protein and carbohydrates will be lost to the cooking water; however, if you are making soup, this doesn't apply, as the cooking liquid is part of the dish, so it can be added at the outset.

Next, bring the pan to the boil and continue to boil for 10 minutes before turning down the heat to a gentle simmer for the remainder of the cooking time.

The preliminary boiling is especially important for red kidney beans, butter/lima beans, borlotti and white beans, in order to destroy the indigestible oligosaccharides which produce gas and the haemagglutinins that can cause food poisoning (see pages 13–14 for more information on this subject.) Chickpeas and lentils do not require this preliminary boiling.

Add any herbs, spices or other flavourings to the pan, but do not add salt at this stage as it has the effect of preventing the beans from softening. Also, don't add any acidic ingredients such as tomatoes, wine or vinegar at this point, as they will slow down or even arrest the cooking process. Sauces containing such ingredients should be added only when the beans are already cooked. This can be an advantage in certain situations, however, as once the beans have been cooked to perfection in water, they can be combined with a tomato-rich sauce which can be allowed to cool and later reheated without the beans breaking down into a mush.

Bring back to the boil, cover the pan and simmer very gently until cooked. Remember to keep checking the water level during cooking and make sure the beans are submerged, adding more hot water if necessary.

Cooking times

It is impossible to give exact timings for cooking pulses/legumes, as so much depends not only on the type, but also on the age of the dried seeds. All will cook more quickly in soft water than hard. The following is a rough guideline for the initial cooking. Further cooking with other ingredients may be required afterwards, according to the recipe.

Split lentils: 20–30 minutes
Whole lentils: 30 minutes–1 hour
Mung beans: 25–45 minutes
Split peas: 1 hour
Black-eyed beans/peas: 1–1½ hours
Split broad/fava beans: 1–2 hours
Other beans and whole peas: 1–3 hours
Chickpeas: 1½–3 hours

Pressure cookers and slow cookers

The use of a pressure cooker can reduce cooking times dramatically and is a worthwhile investment for the regular bean eater.

The constant, gentle heat of an electric slow cooker is perfect for cooking pulses/legumes, but to destroy the toxins, be sure to boil the soaked beans briskly on the hob/stovetop for 10 minutes before slow cooking, as most slow cookers operate at below boiling point. This isn't a problem for pressure cookers, which operate at high enough temperatures to destroy the toxins.

Chapter 1

Soups

Hot and sour Serbian bean soup

Hot, sweet and sour, spiced with paprika and sharpened with a splash of vinegar, this appetizing soup is from the mountains of Serbia, where it is known as *pasulj*. A similar soup, *bableves*, is popular in Hungary, where it is often made even more substantial by adding smoked ham knuckle or sliced sausage in traditional recipes. A touch of sweetness comes from the inclusion of parsley root, otherwise known as Hamburg parsley, which can be difficult to get hold of. Parsnips, which look rather like parsley root but have a blander flavour, are the next best thing. If using dried beans, they should be taken off the heat when half-cooked, as they are subsequently simmered with the other ingredients for another 40 minutes.

500 g/2½ cups half-cooked, soaked, dried white beans, such as cannellini, or the contents of 2 x 400-g/14-oz. cans, drained

2 carrots, peeled and finely chopped

1 parsnip, peeled and finely chopped

1 onion, very finely chopped

30 g/2 tablespoons duck fat, lard or sunflower oil

3 garlic cloves, crushed to a paste with salt

1 teaspoon smoked paprika/pimentón

½ teaspoon hot paprika

salt and ground black pepper

200 ml/¾ cup sour cream

1–2 teaspoons white wine vinegar

3 tablespoons chopped fresh flat-leaf parsley or dill, to serve

Serves 6

Put the beans in a large saucepan, add the chopped carrots, parsnip and onion, top up with enough water to cover all of the vegetables and bring to the boil. Simmer, covered, for about 30 minutes, until all of the vegetables, including the beans, are soft.

In a smaller saucepan, melt the fat or heat the oil over a low heat and add the crushed garlic and salt paste together with both types of paprika. Cook briefly, taking care not to let the paprika burn, then dilute with a little water and add to the beans. Add more water if the soup is too thick. Stir well, then allow the soup to cook for another 10 minutes or so before seasoning with salt and pepper.

Using a blender, purée the sour cream with a ladleful of hot soup, then stir into the rest of the soup. Add the vinegar, according to taste, stir in the parsley or dill, taste and adjust the seasoning and serve.

Senate bean soup

Bean soup may be the ultimate symbol of poverty, but it also appears in the grandest places. One of these is the US Capitol Building, where bean soup makes a daily appearance on the menu in all of the Senate restaurants. Legend has it that this custom dates back to the day when Joseph Gurney Cannon, Speaker of the House of Representatives from 1903–11, entered the dining room, and on perusing the menu, exclaimed 'Thunderation, I had my mouth set for bean soup! From now on, hot or cold, rain or shine, I want it on the menu every day.' Whatever the truth of the matter, I have it on good authority that bean soup is indeed on the menu to this day, and this is a scaled-down version of the historic recipe.

250 g/1⅓ cups dried cannellini or haricot/navy beans, soaked overnight
1 small uncooked ham hock, smoked or unsmoked (about 400–500 g/1 lb.) or 1 ham bone, soaked overnight if very salty
2 fresh or dried bay leaves
1 large onion, finely chopped
2 garlic cloves, finely chopped
2 celery sticks/ribs, trimmed and diced
200 g/1 cup mashed potatoes
2 tablespoons chopped fresh flat-leaf parsley, plus extra to serve (you can use chopped/snipped chives instead to serve)
salt and ground black pepper

Serves 6

Drain the beans and put in a large saucepan with 1.8 litres/7½ cups of fresh water, the ham hock or bone and bay leaves. Bring to the boil and keep on the boil for 10 minutes, then cover the pan, turn down the heat and continue to simmer very gently for another 2 hours.

Add the chopped onion, garlic and celery and cook for another hour, until the beans are thoroughly cooked and tender. Stir in the mashed potato and parsley approximately 5 minutes before the end of the cooking time.

Remove a cupful of beans from the saucepan and either mash them with a fork or blend to a creamy purée with a blender, then stir into the rest of the soup.

Remove the ham hock or bone from the pan. Discard the skin, gristle and fat, then lift the meat off the bone, chop it into strips and return to the soup. Season to taste with salt and pepper.

Serve hot, sprinkled with the additional chopped parsley, or chives.

Note:

The soup can be allowed to cool so that excess fat can be skimmed off the surface before serving, but this may not be necessary.

Sorrel and bean soup

Pale green in colour and subtly flavoured, this delicate soup can be rustled up in no time by using canned beans. Sorrel is very easy to grow in the garden, and is becoming increasingly available in supermarkets. Its lemony freshness makes it an invaluable ingredient in the kitchen.

30 g/2 tablespoons butter
1 large leek (about 175 g/6 oz. trimmed weight), trimmed and finely chopped
2–3 medium shallots, chopped
1 medium potato, peeled and cubed
1 litre/4 cups chicken or vegetable stock
250 g/1⅓ cups cooked, soaked dried flageolet beans, or the contents of 1 x 400-g/14-oz. can, drained
125 g/4 oz. fresh sorrel leaves, shredded
4 tablespoons single/light cream, plus extra to serve
salt and ground black pepper

Serves 4

Melt the butter in a large saucepan and sweat the leek and shallots together for approximately 10 minutes, being careful not to allow them to brown.

Add the cubes of potato and the stock and bring to the boil, then cover the pan and simmer for around 20 minutes. Add half of the cooked beans and reheat.

Stir the shredded sorrel leaves into the soup and cook for 1–2 minutes, then purée the mixture using a blender. Return to the saucepan, add the remaining whole beans and heat gently.

Stir in the cream, taste and season the soup with salt and black pepper, then reheat very gently and serve with an extra swirl of cream.

Moroccan harira soup

There are a great many recipes for *harira*, traditionally served to break the fast during Ramadan in North Africa, especially in Morocco. The ingredients vary from region to region, but usually include lentils or chickpeas, onions, tomatoes, celery, rice, beaten eggs, fresh herbs such as parsley and coriander/cilantro, spices like cinnamon, saffron, ginger and black pepper, and often a small amount of lamb, chicken or whatever meat is to hand. A squeeze of lemon and a handful of fresh herbs stirred in at the end add a refreshing note. It all depends on what is available. Berber nomads in the Algerian desert make *harira* with nothing but milk, butter, egg and semolina.

3 tablespoons olive oil
1 lamb shank, weighing about
   300 g/10 oz.
125 g/½ cup dried chickpeas
   (garbanzos), soaked for 24
   hours and drained, or the
   contents of ½ x 400-g/14-oz.
   can, drained
125 g/½ cup dried green lentils,
   rinsed and drained
1 onion, finely chopped
3 celery sticks/ribs, trimmed
   and chopped
½ teaspoon ground cinnamon
1 teaspoon ground turmeric
½ teaspoon ground ginger
1 teaspoon saffron strands
1 tablespoon tomato purée/paste
2 tablespoons plain/all-purpose
   flour
3 tablespoons chopped fresh
   flat-leaf parsley
4 tablespoons chopped fresh
   coriander/cilantro
salt and ground black pepper
lemon quarters, to serve

Serves 6

Heat the oil in a large saucepan (a capacity of 2 litres/8½ cups) and brown the lamb on all sides. Add the chickpeas, lentils, onion, celery, spices and tomato purée/paste to the saucepan, then pour in 1.5 litres/6½ cups of water. Stir well. Cover the pan and bring to the boil, then after 10 minutes turn down the heat and simmer everything together for 1½–2 hours, until the chickpeas are tender and the meat is falling off the bone.

Remove the lamb shank from the soup and strip the meat off the bone, then chop the meat and return it to the saucepan.

Whisk the flour into 300 ml/1¼ cups of cold water, blending until it is completely smooth, then stir the mixture into the soup. Bring the soup back to the boil and simmer for 10 minutes to thicken the broth.

Stir in the chopped fresh herbs, season with salt and plenty of black pepper and serve with lemon quarters to squeeze in the soup.

Traditional cooking vessels

Despite the advent of fast-food devices, such as the microwave and the pressure-cooker, there's no denying that the very best bean stews are the result of long, slow cooking in a sealed pot, preferably on the dying embers of a wood fire. For most of us this isn't really an option, but the design of a traditional bean pot has elements that make for perfect cooking even in a modern kitchen.

Like all utensils that are fit for purpose, the bean pot has a particular beauty. Usually made from earthenware, always glazed inside but sometimes unglazed outside, its wide-bellied, narrow-necked shape is a symbol of domestic comfort and the promise of a good meal.

Small wonder that the basic design hasn't changed since the Iron Age – it is just one of those shapes that can't be improved upon. In the past, wooden or tin lids would sometimes be used, or in place of a lid, a small secondary pot containing water would be placed on top of the main pot, ingeniously providing hot water for topping up the contents of the pot below at the same time as reducing evaporation. Later, the addition of a close-fitting lid – which retains all of the moisture by directing the condensed liquids back into the stew, allowing for slow, gentle cooking – became the secret of the best bean casseroles.

The Spanish *olla*, which is commonly used in Mexico and throughout the Hispanic world, strongly resembles those used in the kitchens of ancient Rome, and has hardly changed over the millennia. Traditionally made of earthenware, the Mexican *olla* sometimes has a small *cazuela* that doubles as a lid and a container for hot water, is used to top up the beans in the *olla* below. Another Spanish pot of ancient origin, the *puchero*, has the same pot-bellied shape and has given its name to the meat and chickpea stew that is cooked in it.

Whether the Spanish brought the *olla* to the New World or not is a moot point, but legend has it that native Americans showed the Pilgrim Settlers how to grow and cook the 'holy trinity' of corn, beans and squash, and may well have handed on the shape of the classic bean pot now associated with Boston, and thus with baked beans.

Southern Italy has its own terracotta cooking pot, the *pignata*. This comes from the word *la pigna*, which means pine cone, as its shape is upright and conical, more like a jug/pitcher with two handles placed on one side so that it could be positioned close to the fire without the cook getting burned. In the well-known Italian cookbook *Honey from a Weed*, the author Patience Gray describes how in Puglia, the winter staples – beans and chickpeas – were cooked in these *pignate*, which were lidless and therefore required topping up with hot liquid from time to time. She describes how two jars would be used, one half-filled with the selected legume, then filled up with cold cistern water and a pinch of bicarbonate of/baking soda, while the other jar would provide boiling water for topping up the bean pot during cooking.

Similar unlidded vessels are found in the French Vendée, where white *mogette* beans are the local speciality. They were once cooked in earthenware vessels at the side of the fire and are now served in restaurants in these one-handled pots as a reminder of times past.

Northern Italy also has its *pignatta*, this one with a lid and more squat in shape than the Puglian one. The town of Castellamonte is famous for its *pignatta*, a lovely four-handled bean pot made from local red clay, and used to cook *la tofeja*, a rich stew of speckled Saluggia beans with pork skin.

Another beautifully designed bean pot, the *idra*, existed in the days of the Egyptian pharaohs and is still in use today. Made of earthenware, it has a conical lid, shaped rather like a tagine, and is the traditional cooking pot for *ful medames*, the national dish of long-simmered dried broad/fava beans. As steam condenses on the inside of the lid, it drops down into the pot and keeps the contents moist during the long cooking. In this way the dish can be economically prepared on the small electric hotplate found in most Egyptian kitchens.

But the most bizarre of bean-cooking vessels is the Tuscan *fiasco*, a flask made of glass. When I saw these for sale in a hardware shop in Lucca, I could hardly believe that they could be used for cooking. Modern versions are made of Pyrex, but in days gone by, when Chianti wine came in flask-shaped bottles, these were used to cook cannellini beans on the dying embers of the wood fire or in the bread oven after a day of baking. The long, slow cooking – 5–6 hours minimum – and the traditional seasonings of sage, garlic and olive oil make this an exceptionally appealing dish. However, it is tempting to surmise that the origin of the current meaning of the word 'fiasco' may have been the result of the inevitable accidents that must have occurred, although there is no evidence for this.

Another traditional bean pot, the French *cassole*, should be mentioned as it gave its name to cassoulet, possibly the most famous dish in French country cooking. The dish is open, wide at the top and tapering down at the base. It is used only for the final stages of preparing cassoulet, when the various meats are cooked to succulence and have released their fat, which rises to the surface and is amalgamated into the coating of breadcrumbs on top of the dish. The preliminary cooking of the beans and meat, however, would probably be done using a lidded *marmite*, a word that has become synonymous with the well-known yeast extract rather than French country cooking.

Armenian lentil soup with apricots

Apricots are a big deal in Armenia. Even their scientific name, *Prunus armeniaca*, suggests that the fruit is a native of Armenia, although some believe it originated in China. The July harvest is celebrated in the country's capital, Yerevan, with an annual festival, and the international film festival held here is named 'The Golden Apricot', in honour of their national fruit. This mellow soup is typical of Armenian cuisine; the apricot gives a touch of acidity, but you may like to squeeze lemon juice in at the end as well.

2 tablespoons sunflower oil
1 onion, chopped
1 green, red or yellow (bell)
    pepper, deseeded and chopped
1 teaspoon ground cumin
½ teaspoon ground cinnamon
½ teaspoon cayenne pepper
1 teaspoon paprika, hot or sweet,
    according to preference
200 g/1 cup dried red lentils,
    rinsed and drained
100 g/⅔ cup dried apricots
1 large waxy potato, peeled
    and diced
1.75 litres/7 cups vegetable stock
salt and ground black pepper
2 tablespoons chopped fresh
    flat-leaf parsley, to garnish
plain yogurt, to serve
lemon wedges, to serve

Serves 4

Heat the oil in a saucepan, and gently cook the onion and (bell) pepper. When both are soft, stir in the spices and cook for 1–2 minutes to release the aromas.

While the vegetables are cooking, place the lentils, apricots, diced potato and stock in a large saucepan and bring to the boil, then simmer for 30 minutes.

Blend the soup in a blender, then taste and adjust the seasoning. If the soup seems too thick, thin it down with water and reheat.

Stir in the onion and pepper mixture, and serve with a dollop of yogurt swirled into the centre of each bowl, the chopped parsley strewn over the top and the lemon wedges on the side.

Lentil and chestnut soup from Abruzzo

This is mountain food for autumn/fall – rich and comforting, yet simplicity
itself to assemble. If possible, choose lentils from the mountains of Umbria
or Abruzzo, or from the volcanic French region of Le Puy, as these have the
most flavour and don't completely disintegrate on cooking, giving the soup
a pleasant texture. Chestnuts, as well as lentils, are prepared to put up with
poor soils and harsh climates, and they combine perfectly with lentils,
adding a sweet mealiness that is very soothing.

30 g/2 tablespoons duck or goose
   fat, lard or olive oil
1 onion, chopped
2 carrots, peeled and diced
2 celery sticks/ribs, trimmed
   and diced
3 garlic cloves, chopped
250 g/8 oz. dried Puy/French
   green lentils, rinsed and
   drained
1 fresh or dried bay leaf
1 teaspoon fennel seeds, crushed
2 sprigs of fresh thyme or
   1 teaspoon dried thyme
200 g/7 oz. cooked and peeled
   chestnuts (canned or bottled
   are fine, but chestnuts roasted
   over a fire would be best)
1 tablespoon tomato purée/paste
4 tablespoons chopped fresh
   flat-leaf parsley
salt and ground black pepper
good olive oil, to serve

Serves 6–8

Heat the cooking fat, lard or olive oil in a large saucepan. Add the
onion, carrots, celery and garlic and soften gently for approximately
10 minutes, until the vegetables are giving off a pleasant fragrance
and the onion is golden in colour.

Add the drained lentils, the bay leaf, the fennel seeds and thyme,
cover with 1.5 litres/6½ cups of water, cover the pan and simmer for
30 minutes or so. Chop the chestnuts roughly and add them to the
pan together with the tomato purée/paste and seasoning. Continue to
cook for another 20–30 minutes, until the soup is thick enough and
the lentils are thoroughly cooked. Dilute with extra water if the soup
seems too thick.

Stir in the chopped parsley, season with salt and pepper and serve hot
with some good olive oil to drizzle over the surface of the soup.

Potage Saint-Germain
(French split pea soup)

The city of Paris was once surrounded by market gardens which supplied the inhabitants with fresh vegetables, and the suburb Faubourg Saint-Germain was famous for its peas.

250 g/1⅓ cups dried green split peas, preferably soaked overnight★
1 fresh or dried bay leaf
60 g/4 tablespoons butter
1 onion, chopped
2 leeks, trimmed and chopped
2 garlic cloves, finely chopped
175 g/1¼ cups frozen peas (or fresh if available)
60 ml/½ cup single/light cream
salt and ground black pepper
croutons, to serve
a few fresh mint leaves, to serve

Serves 6

Drain the split peas and put in a large saucepan with the bay leaf and 1.5 litres/6½ cups of fresh water. Bring to the boil, then simmer until cooked – around 30 minutes.

While the peas are cooking, melt the butter in another saucepan and gently sweat the onion and leeks until soft. Add the garlic and continue to cook for 1–2 minutes.

When the split peas are thoroughly cooked, remove and discard the bay leaf, then transfer the peas and their cooking liquid into the pan with the softened onion, leeks and garlic.

Cook the frozen (or fresh) peas for 1 minute in a separate saucepan of boiling water, drain and add them to the other ingredients. (If you prefer a soup with some texture, put only half of the peas in at this stage, adding the other half just before serving.)

Purée the soup using a blender, adding the cream right at the end. Return to the pan, then season to taste, stir in the mint, reheat and serve with croutons.

★ If the green split peas have not been soaked overnight, they will take 1 hour or so to cook, rather than 30 minutes.

Broad bean soup for springtime

This is a lovely soup for spring, which uses up the last of the winter's supply of dried fava beans and incorporates the new season's crop to lighten the look and taste of the soup. They also bring a pleasing texture to the smooth base of the soup. Peeling broad/fava beans may seem like a good way to waste time, but it doesn't take long, and is peculiarly satisfying, watching the brilliant green kernels pop out of their wrinkly, tough outer skins. If the beans are rather old, this is definitely worth doing, but small, tender beans can be left intact. Although the bright colour of the fresh beans dulls fairly quickly, this soup still tastes just as good the next day.

2 tablespoons olive oil
1 onion, chopped
2 celery sticks, trimmed and
    chopped
175 g/1 scant cup skinned and
    split dried fava beans
1 litre/4 cups vegetable stock or
    water
winter or summer savory, dried
    or fresh (optional)
150 g/1 cup shelled broad/fava
    beans, fresh or frozen
3 tomatoes
a handful of fresh mint, chopped
salt and ground black pepper

Serves 4

Add the oil to a saucepan and soften the onion and celery over a gentle heat to avoid browning.

When soft, add the dried fava beans to the pan, stir around, then add the stock or water, and winter or summer savory if you have it. Cover and bring to the boil, then keep on the boil for 10 minutes. Turn down the heat and simmer for a further 20–50 minutes, or until the beans have broken down into a mush.

Meanwhile, bring a pan of water to the boil, and blanch the fresh or frozen broad/fava beans for 1 minute, then remove them using a slotted spoon and skin them if the skins are tough. Scald the tomatoes in the same pan of boiling water, then skin and chop them.

Purée the dried bean and celery mixture using a blender until smooth, then return to the pan, stir in the fresh beans, tomato and mint and reheat. Season to taste and serve.

Cuban black bean and red pepper soup

This is a substantial soup, almost a main course, that combines the sweetness of red peppers with the heat of red chilli/chile in the accompanying salsa.

200 g/1 cup dried black beans, soaked overnight, or the contents of 2 x 400-g/14-oz. cans, drained
1 litre/4 cups water
1 small onion, peeled
1 small green (bell) pepper, cut in half and deseeded
1 fresh or dried bay leaf

For the sofrito
3 tablespoons olive oil
2 garlic cloves, chopped
1 onion, roughly chopped
1 green (bell) pepper, deseeded and chopped
4 red or yellow (bell) peppers, 2 deseeded and chopped and 2 cut in half and deseeded
1 teaspoon ground cumin
1 teaspoon dried oregano
1 fresh or dried bay leaf
½ tablespoon red wine vinegar
salt and sugar, to taste
crème fraîche or sour cream, to serve

For the salsa
1–2 fresh hot red chillies/chiles, stalks removed and deseeded
1 shallot, chopped
3 garlic cloves, peeled
2 tablespoons white wine vinegar
4 ripe tomatoes, skinned and chopped
½ teaspoon ground cumin
½ teaspoon dried oregano
2 tablespoons chopped fresh coriander/cilantro
salt and sugar, to taste

In a large saucepan, add the beans with all of their other ingredients, cover and bring to the boil, then turn down the heat and simmer for about 1½ hours, or until soft. If using canned beans, cook for only 30 minutes. When they are cooked, discard the onion, (bell) pepper and bay leaf, then transfer a ladleful of beans to a bowl and mash them.

While the beans are cooking, make the sofrito. Heat the oil in another pan and fry the garlic for a few seconds, then tip in the onion and chopped red or yellow (bell) peppers and fry over a low heat until soft. Add the cumin, oregano and bay leaf and cook for a few minutes together.

Roast the halved red or yellow (bell) peppers directly over a gas flame or under a grill/broiler, skin-side towards the heat source. When the skin is blackened all over, place the peppers in a plastic bag for a few minutes. Take them out, remove the skin and chop the flesh.

Stir the mashed beans into the sofrito. Add the remaining cooked beans with their liquid and stir in the vinegar, sugar and salt (about ½ teaspoon of sugar and 1 teaspoon of salt should be just about right.) Combine the skinned and chopped red or yellow (bell) peppers with the rest of the soup and simmer everything together for a few minutes.

For the salsa, in a food processor, pulse the chilli/chile, shallot, garlic and vinegar to a purée. Add the chopped tomatoes, cumin and herbs and pulse again briefly. Season with salt and sugar to taste.

Serve the soup with a dollop of crème fraîche or sour cream and one of salsa.

Serves 4–6

London Particular (Pea and ham soup)

This soup has a curious history. Don't let the name put you off what is truly a delightful soup. It refers to the dense, greenish smog – known initially as a 'pea-souper', but later as a 'London Particular' – that frequently plagued London from the start of the Industrial Revolution in the late 18th century to the introduction of the Clean Air Act in 1956. If the ham hock is very salty, soak it in water overnight before using, and discard the water.

30 g/2 tablespoons butter
1 onion, chopped
1 celery stick/rib, trimmed and
    chopped
1 large carrot, peeled and
    chopped
400 g/2 cups dried green or
    yellow split peas, preferably
    soaked overnight and drained
1 small ham hock
    (approximately 500 g/1 lb.)
salt and ground black pepper

Serves 4

Melt the butter in a large saucepan and fry the onion, celery and carrot until soft. Add the drained split peas to the pan, together with the ham hock and 1.8 litres/7½ cups of water. Cover and bring to the boil, then turn down the heat and simmer for about 2½ hours, or until the meat is falling off the bone and the peas are breaking down into the liquid.

Remove the ham hock from the pan, strip off the skin, gristle and fat, lift the meat off the bone and cut into bite-sized chunks.

If you like the soup smooth, blend it to a purée using a blender, then return it to the pan, add the ham and reheat. Otherwise, just return the ham chunks to the pan, season to taste and serve.

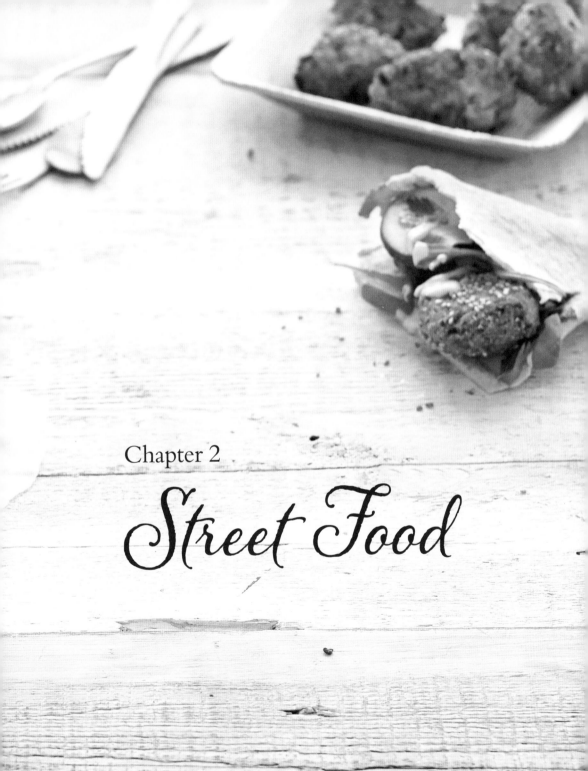

Chapter 2

Street Food

Chickpea fritters

In Sicily, chickpea/gram flour is boiled with water to make a thick batter, allowed to cool, then cut into squares and fried into irresistible soft-yet-crunchy fritters called *panelle*. Best eaten hot, they are often served in a sesame bun, like a burger. In Liguria, *pizzerie* sell a similar street snack, called *panissa* or *panizza*, while over the border in Nice, where they are known as *panisses*, where the batter is usually poured into saucers, cooled and cut into batons, much like chunky fries.

200 g/1½ cups chickpea/gram
   flour, sifted
1 teaspoon salt
1 tablespoon chopped fresh
   flat-leaf parsley
3 tablespoons olive oil
coarse sea salt and ground black
   pepper

Serves 4-6

Whisk the chickpea/gram flour into 600 ml/2½ cups of water until there are no lumps, then season with the salt.

Heat the batter gently in a saucepan, stirring constantly, until it boils and thickens. Simmer the mixture for about 15 minutes, whisking constantly, as lumps tend to form otherwise. Stir in the parsley and cook for another 5 minutes.

Working quickly, poor onto oiled baking sheet about 34 x 24 cm (14 x 10 in.), and smooth out the surface. Cover with a sheet of silicone or baking paper and using a rolling pin, roll out to flatten the surface. The mixture should be about 6 mm/¾ in. thick. Leave to cool for several hours to allow the mixture to solidify.

Preheat the oven to 200°C (400°F) Gas 6. When the batter has cooled and solidified, cut into triangles, squares or, to make chunky chips, batons about the size of your largest finger.

When the oven is hot, put the olive oil in a clean baking sheet and heat in the oven for a few minutes, then using a spatula, transfer the triangles, squares or batons to the hot oil, flipping over once to coat both sides with oil. Put in the oven for about 20 minutes, until the *panelle* are crisp on the surface and starting to brown, then turn over and cook for another 10 minutes.

Alternatively, heat some oil in a frying pan/skillet, and fry the *panelle* on the hob/stovetop.

Sprinkle with coarse sea salt and black pepper and serve immediately, either as a snack with drinks or with a salad.

Black lentil pancakes with mint raita

Black beluga lentils are best for these little pancakes, as they hold their shape well when cooked. Puy lentils could also be used, as an alternative.

125 g/⅔ cup dried black beluga lentils, rinsed and drained
75 g/⅔ cup plain/all-purpose flour
1 egg
150 ml/⅔ cup milk
1 teaspoon ground cumin
½–1 teaspoon salt
1–2 dried red chillies/chiles, deseeded and finely chopped
2 tablespoons chopped coriander/cilantro leaves
vegetable oil, for frying

For the raita:

300 ml/1¼ cups plain yogurt
6-cm/2½-in. piece of cucumber, peeled and grated
2 tablespoons chopped fresh mint, plus whole leaves to garnish
¼ teaspoon ground cumin
salt and ground black pepper

Makes about 20

Put the lentils in a large saucepan with enough water to cover them, cover the pan and bring to the boil, then turn down the heat and simmer for 25–30 minutes, until tender. Drain and set aside.

Whisk together the flour, egg, milk, cumin and salt until smooth. Stir in the cooked lentils, the chopped chillies/chiles and the coriander/cilantro and set aside.

Make the raita by beating the yogurt until smooth and then stirring in the other ingredients.

Heat a tablespoon of oil in a large frying pan/skillet or pancake pan. To make bite-sized pancakes, drop scant tablespoonfuls of the batter onto the hot pan/skillet, smoothing out the surface of each as you go. You should be able to make 6–7 at a time. Cook over a medium heat for approximately 5 minutes, until the undersides are beginning to brown, then turn over with a spatula and cook the other side. Continue until all of the batter is used.

Good to nibble on with drinks, they are best served warm with a teaspoonful of mint raita on each pancake and a mint leaf to garnish.

Shallot and banana bhajis

These delectable, crunchy morsels are best served as soon as they come out of the pan, and make a good snack to nibble with drinks, especially alongside a bowl of sweet and sour tamarind or coriander/cilantro chutney as a dip. Other ingredients such as chopped spring onions/scallions, fenugreek leaves, spinach or grated carrot can be incorporated into the bhaji mix, depending on what is available. The chickpea/gram flour acts as a binder for the other ingredients and gives a lovely crisp texture.

175 g/a scant 1½ cups chickpea/
   gram flour, sifted
2 shallots, finely chopped
1 potato (about 100 g/3½ oz.),
   peeled and grated
1 teaspoon chopped fresh ginger
1 teaspoon chopped fresh green
   chilli/chile, or more to taste
½ teaspoon chilli powder
½ unripe banana, chopped
¾ teaspoon salt
vegetable oil, for frying

Serves 4

Mix all of the ingredients apart from the oil in a bowl and add just enough water (about 200 ml/a generous ¾ cup) to make a mixture that holds together and can be dropped off a spoon.

In a medium-sized saucepan, heat enough oil to deep fry about 6 small bhajis at a time. The oil should be hot enough to brown a cube of bread in 30 seconds (around 180°–190°C/360°–375°F).

When it is hot enough, use a teaspoon and a dessert spoon to drop walnut-sized balls of the mixture into the oil. Cook over a medium heat until golden brown, turning over as they cook, then remove them with a slotted spoon and drain on paper towels. Cook the rest of the bhajis in the same way, 5–6 at a time, draining on paper towels while you fry the next batch.

The bhajis are best served straight away, but can be cooked in advance and reheated if that is more convenient.

Brazilian black-eyed bean and prawn fritters

These fritters are known as *acarajé* in Brazil, and are a popular snack of the Bahia region in the north of the country. They are traditionally sold by white-robed women with colourful headdresses. A similar falafel-like snack called *akara* can be found in Nigeria.

200 g/1 cup dried black-eyed beans/peas, soaked overnight and drained
1 onion, chopped
2 fresh chillies/chiles, red or green, chopped
½ teaspoon fish sauce
1 egg white, lightly beaten
1 teaspoon salt
125 g/4 oz. peeled prawns/shrimp, chopped
vegetable oil, for frying

For the salsa:

1 red onion, finely chopped
1 tomato, skinned and chopped
1 garlic clove, finely chopped
2 tablespoons olive oil
1 tablespoon freshly squeezed lime juice
1 fresh chilli/chile, green or red, finely chopped
1 tablespoon chopped fresh coriander/cilantro
salt and ground black pepper

Makes about 24

Put the black-eyed bean/peas in a saucepan, cover with 3 times their volume of water and bring to the boil. Simmer for 2 minutes, then take the pan off the heat and leave to soak in the water for 4 hours. Drain off the water and put the beans/peas into a food processor. Pulse briefly to break the skins, then add enough water to cover them and pulse again. Some of the beans/peas will break up, but that doesn't matter. Transfer the beans/peas and water to a large bowl and put in the sink. Rub the beans/peas vigorously with your fingers to loosen the skins, then put the pan under the cold tap/faucet, swishing the beans around so that the skins rise to the surface and can be skimmed off and discarded. Drain the beans/peas thoroughly when most of the skins have gone.

In a food processor, blend the beans/peas, onion, chilli/chile, fish sauce, egg white and salt with 125 ml/½ cup of water to make a paste. Add the chopped prawns/shrimp and mix well to incorporate them, then cover and leave this batter in the fridge for 1 hour.

Mix all of the salsa ingredients together in a bowl.

Heat the oil in a saucepan – it should be at least 5 cm/2 in. deep so that the fritters are covered. When the oil is hot, slip dessert-spoonfuls of the batter into the hot oil and fry in batches until golden brown on all sides, making sure they are fully cooked through. Drain on paper towels and serve hot with the salsa.

Indian lentil and rice dosas

These lacy thin pancakes are often eaten for breakfast in India, so the 32-hour preparation process starts in the evening. A simple potato and pea curry makes a good filling for dosas, served with fresh coriander/cilantro and mint chutney.

350 g/1¾ cups basmati rice, rinsed and drained
125 g/⅔ cup white urid dal, rinsed and drained
1 teaspoon fenugreek seeds
spring or bottled water (not tap/faucet water, as it contains chlorine)
1–2 teaspoons salt
vegetable oil, for frying
potato and pea curry, to serve
fresh coriander/cilantro and mint chutney, to serve

Makes about 12

Put the rice and dal in separate bowls, adding the fenugreek seeds to the dal. Cover each with spring or bottled water by 5 cm/2 in. and leave to soak for 8 hours. After soaking, drain the dal, retaining the soaking water, and grind the dal and fenugreek in a food processor to a fine paste. Add 100 ml/⅓ cup of the soaking water to the paste and blend again, to achieve a smooth batter. Pour into a large bowl.

Repeat the process with the rice, grinding to a fine grainy texture, then add 125 ml/½ cup of the soaking water and blend again. Pour the rice batter into the bowl with the dal and mix thoroughly. Add another 250 ml/1 cup of water and mix again. The batter should be the consistency of single/light cream and should coat the back of a spoon dipped into the mixture. Cover the bowl with clingfilm/plastic wrap and set aside in a warm place to ferment for 24 hours.

When ready to make the pancakes, stir the batter, which will be frothy by now, and add the salt. It may be necessary to add more water, but it is better to make a trial pancake first.

Heat a frying pan/skillet or pancake pan, preferably non-stick, and brush with oil. Wipe off the excess oil with a paper towel. When the pan is medium hot, lift a ladleful onto the centre of the pan/skillet, then quickly spread the batter as thinly as possible, using the back of the ladle, moving it around in a spiral, starting at the centre of the pan/skillet. This has to be done quite quickly, before the batter starts to cook. The pancakes should be at least 20 cm/8 in. in diameter – if the batter doesn't spread that far, add a little more water to the bowl.

When the edges start to look lacy and crisp, gently lift the edge of the pancake to see if it is cooked and golden brown underneath. At this stage a little extra oil can be drizzled round the edge of the pan/skillet. Using a spatula, turn over the dosa and cook on the other side for a few minutes. Keep the pancakes warm as you make them, piled on a plate covered with kitchen foil.

Serve each one with a spoonful of potato and pea curry spread across the centre. Spoon some fresh coriander/cilantro and mint chutney on top, and fold the pancake over from either side to seal.

Korean moong pancakes with pork

These savoury pancakes often contain kimchi, the Korean spiced pickled cabbage that is becoming increasingly popular around the world, but this version uses green beans instead. Either way, they make a delicious snack.

400 g/2 cups dried moong dal (skinned and split mung beans), soaked overnight
2 tablespoons soy sauce, plus extra to serve
4 garlic cloves, crushed
1 tablespoon grated fresh ginger
4 tablespoons vegetable oil
250 g/8 oz. minced/ground lean pork
1 teaspoon salt
1 leek, trimmed and finely chopped
125 g/4 oz. green beans, fresh or frozen, chopped into small pieces
chopped pickled cucumber and sliced red chilli/chile (optional), to serve

Makes about 12

Drain the moong dal and put them in the food processor. Blend them finely, then add 400 ml/1⅔ cups of water, the soy sauce, all but 1 crushed garlic clove and all but ½ teaspoon of the grated ginger. Process the mixture to a smooth purée.

Heat 2 tablespoons of the oil in a frying pan/skillet or wok and fry the remaining garlic for 1 minute before adding the pork, together with the remaining ½ teaspoon of grated ginger and salt. Stir well and continue to cook until the pork is cooked through, then add the chopped leek and green beans and continue to cook gently until the vegetables are half-cooked, but not soft. Take off the heat and set aside.

Transfer the moong dal purée to a bowl, then leave the batter to sit for at least 30 minutes.

Heat a teaspoon of oil in a non-stick frying pan/skillet over a medium heat, and when it is hot, pour a spoonful of the batter into the pan/skillet. Spread out the batter with the back of the ladle until it forms a 8-cm/3-in. circle. Repeat the process with more batter, frying several pancakes at a time.

Cook the pancakes until golden brown on the underside and until tiny holes have begun to appear on the upper surface, then flip them over and cook the other side. This will probably take around 5 minutes on each side. It is important not to overheat the pan and burn the surface before the inside is cooked, but it must be hot enough for the pancakes to brown and crisp.

Keep warm while you make the other pancakes in the same way, brushing the frying pan/skillet or wok with oil before cooking each batch. Serve straight away with a bowl of soy sauce for dipping, and pickled cucumber and some sliced red chilli/chile, if desired.

Fava bean falafel

The perfect street food, falafel have been enjoyed in the Middle East for generations, but it's only recently that Europeans have caught on to this healthy vegetarian alternative to the burger. They are at their best when freshly cooked and served with tahini sauce. In Israel, falafel are usually made with chickpeas, but in Egypt, where they are thought to have originated, they are made with dried split fava beans, as in this recipe, and are called *ta'amia*.

350 g/2 cups split dried fava beans, soaked overnight
2 garlic cloves, finely chopped
2 teaspoons ground cumin
2 teaspoons ground coriander
a pinch of chilli powder
½ teaspoon baking powder
1–2 teaspoons salt
1 tablespoon chopped fresh flat-leaf parsley
2 tablespoons chopped fresh coriander/cilantro
8 spring onions/scallions, trimmed and finely chopped
3 tablespoons sesame seeds
vegetable oil, for deep frying
warmed pitta bread and salad, to serve

For the tahini sauce:

2 tablespoons tahini
4 tablespoons water
grated zest and freshly squeezed juice of 1 lemon
4 tablespoons olive oil
1 garlic clove, crushed to a paste with a pinch of salt

Serves 4–6

Drain the fava beans and tip them onto a tea/dish towel to dry them. Then put them into a food processor and grind them to a smooth paste. Add the garlic, spices, baking powder and salt and pulse again briefly before adding the chopped herbs and spring onions/scallions. Process again briefly, then transfer the mixture to a bowl, cover and leave in the fridge for about 1 hour.

Meanwhile, make the tahini sauce by simply whisking together all of the ingredients thoroughly. Place in the fridge.

Next, wet your hands and use them to form the chilled bean mixture into little patties about 5 cm/2 in. across and 2 cm/¾ in. thick. The amount given should make about 16–20 patties.

Spread the sesame seeds onto a plate and gently press each patty into the seeds to coat both sides.

In a saucepan, heat enough oil to completely submerge a patty. When the oil is hot enough to sizzle when a cube of bread is dropped in, carefully transfer a batch of patties into the hot oil, one at a time, then fry them for about 5 minutes, until deep golden brown all over. You may need to turn them over during cooking once or twice to get an even brown colour and to ensure that they are thoroughly cooked. As they cook, remove the patties and drain on paper towels, then keep warm while you fry the rest.

Serve the falafel in split pockets of warmed pitta bread, with slices of cucumber and tomato, salad leaves and tahini sauce drizzled over.

Georgian bean pies

Served as an appetizer or snack, these pies are a classic feature of Georgian cooking; a cheese-filled variant is a popular street food in Georgia's capital, Tbilisi.

50 g/3 tablespoons unsalted butter, chilled and diced
250 g/2 cups self-raising/rising flour
1 egg
½ teaspoon salt
75 ml/⅓ cup buttermilk or plain yogurt
milk, for brushing
melted butter, for brushing

For the filling:

50 g/3 tablespoons butter
2 tablespoons olive oil
1 large onion, finely chopped
2 teaspoons ground coriander
250 g/1¼ cups cooked, soaked dried red kidney beans, or the contents of 1 x 400-g/14-oz. can, drained
150 g/5 oz. feta cheese, crumbled (optional)
3 tablespoons fresh chopped coriander/cilantro leaves
½ teaspoon salt
ground black pepper

Makes 2

Rub the butter into the flour using your fingers, or pulse in a food processor, until the mixture resembles breadcrumbs. Beat the egg, salt and the buttermilk or yogurt together and stir into the flour, then gather the dough together and press it into a ball. If necessary, add some extra buttermilk or yogurt, but don't worry if the mixture seems a bit crumbly. Wrap in clingfilm/plastic wrap and leave to rest in the fridge for about 30 minutes while you make the filling.

Preheat the oven to 180°C (350°F) Gas 4.

Melt the butter with the olive oil and sauté the onions over a medium heat for about 30 minutes, or until nicely browned. Stir from time to time to prevent them from burning. Add the ground coriander and cook gently for another 5 minutes.

Rinse and drain the beans, then mash them or blend briefly in a food processor, taking care not to overprocess them – a roughish texture is desirable. If using, the crumbled feta cheese can be added at this point, before stirring in the chopped coriander/cilantro.

When the onions are cooked, stir them into the bean paste and season with the salt and some black pepper.

Oil a large baking sheet and place in the oven to heat.

Take the dough out of the fridge and divide it into quarters. On a floured board, roll each quarter out into a circle, aiming to get 2 of them about 20 cm/8 in. in diameter, and the others 18 cm/7 in. Trim off any uneven bits to get the shape roughly circular. Alternatively, roll the pastry out thinly and cut smaller circles to make individual pies, folded over to form semi-circles.

Spoon half of the bean mixture onto the centre of each of the larger circles of dough, and spread out evenly, leaving a border around the edge. Brush some milk around the edge of each. Place the smaller circles on top of each pie, and fold the bottom borders over the top, pressing down lightly at even intervals to stick the edges together and seal in the beans.

Take the hot baking sheet out of the oven and one at a time, carefully place the pies onto the sheet. Brush them with melted butter. Bake for about 30 minutes (or 20 minutes for the individual pies), until the pastry is golden brown. Leave to cool slightly before serving.

Bean Festivals

Santa Pau

Every year, the tiny Catalan village of Santa Pau holds a bean festival, La Fira del Fesol, on a Sunday in late January. It's a big event for such a small village. The carnival atmosphere hits you immediately - market stalls line the streets, piled high with local produce: ham, chunky slabs of bacon, sausages of all shapes and sizes, black pudding, pork scratchings, country bread and *coca* (Catalan flatbread topped with pine nuts), buckwheat bread and cakes, all kinds of cheeses and huge cauldrons of cooked beans. Small and white and very similar to haricot/navy beans in appearance, they have sustained the peasant farmers of the Garrotxa region for centuries, together with chestnut, buckwheat and other mountain staples. The Garrotxa, in the foothills of the Pyrenees, is a region of extinct volcanoes, and it's the volcanic soil that reputedly gives the beans the uniquely silky-smooth texture for which they are so highly prized. The genuine article is in short supply and sells for around 7€ per kilo.

This is the chance for local chefs to shine, after weeks of perfecting their recipes. Among the many offerings are Santa Pau beans with crumbled pork sausage or tripe or snails, and pancakes stuffed with beans and squid. The ubiquitous use of the Catalan language adds to the general mystery and excitement of the tasting.

The main event is the *fesolada*, or bean tasting, held to the sound of troubadour music – bagpipes, flutes and drums – which seems entirely in keeping with the medieval origins of Santa Pau. The town's two interlinked squares fill up with smiling people, happy to bump into old friends and enjoy the conviviality of the festival as well as the food and drink. The patron saint of the *fira*, Sant Antoni, is brought out of the church for the occasion, together with his pig, and surveys the scene with amusement.

Le Poiré-sur-Vie

The Vendée region in western France is home to some special white beans, known as *les mogettes*. On 14th August, at the time when the demi-sec harvest is taking place, the town of Le-Poiré-sur-Vie hosts a festival, La Nuit de la Mogette.

As early as 9.30 in the morning, the cooks start lighting wood fires and putting vast cauldrons of beans, which have been soaking overnight, on to boil. Very little seasoning is added to the cooking water – just cloves of garlic, sprigs of rosemary and a few bay leaves, but no salt. As the fires get going, smoke starts to rise, and this is said by some to flavour the beans. Certainly the smell is hugely atmospheric. Because of the size of the pans, it takes a very long time to get the beans to boiling point, but once boiling, about 2 hours' gentle simmering is usually enough to cook them to the point at which they are soft, just beginning to collapse but not falling apart completely. In all, 250 kg/550 lbs. of dried beans are cooked and served on this one day, enough, apparently, to feed 4,000 people. All day, the cooks are at work, feeding the fires, moving pots around to ensure all simmer at just the right temperature and giving the occasional stir.

By early evening, the first portions of the main event – *mogettes* and ham – are being served, accompanied by chunky slices of country bread, toasted on the embers of the wood fires. Food could hardly be plainer than this – the beans are unadorned, the slices of ham simply grilled. Such is the pleasure Vendéens take in their local produce, they see no need to mess it up with fancy sauces or other concoctions.

The celebrations continue into the night, with music and dancing, like a traditional French fête, finishing with an impressive firework display.

FESTIVAL	WHEN	WHERE	DETAILS
Fagiolata di San Defendente	January 2nd	Castiglione d'Asti, Piedmont, Italy	www.castiglioneasti.it
Fagiolata di San Giulio	Last Sunday in January	Bellinzago Novarese, Novara, Piemonte, Italy	www.comune.bellinzago.no.it
La Fira del Fesol de Santa Pau (White Bean Festival)	Late January, La Fira de Sant Antoni	Santa Pau, Girona, Spain	www.santapau.com
Zolfino Bean Festival	End of April–beginning May	Terrranuova Bracciolini, Arezzo, Italy	
La Nuit de la Mogette	August	Le Poiré-sur-Vie, Vendée, France	www.vendée.fr
La Fête de la Lentille	August	Rosières, Haute Loire, France	
Sagra del Fagioli di Sorana	Late August	Sorana, Tuscany, Italy	www.fagiolodisorana.org
Sagra del Fagiolo di Sarconi	Last part of August	Sarconi, Potenza, Basilicata, Italy	www.prolocosarconi.org
National Lentil Festival	Late August	Pullman, Washington, USA	www.lentilfest.com
Zurich Bean Fest	Late August/early September	Zurich, Ontario, Canada	http://beanfest.ca
Michigan Bean Festival	Late August/early September	Fairgrove, Michigan, USA	www.michiganbeanfestival.com
La Fête des Lentilles	Beginning of September	Heimsbrunn, Alsace, France	www.prolocosutri.it
Sagra del Fagiolo	1st/2nd weekend in September	Sutri, Viterbo, Lazio, Italy	
La Fête de la Lentille Verte du Berry	2nd weekend in September	Vatan, Indre, France	
Festa del Fagiolo Lamon	3rd weekend in September	Lamon, Belluno, Veneto, Italy	http://www.prolocolamon.it/index.php/festafagiolo
Lima Bean Festival	October	West Cape May, New Jersey, USA	www.westcapemaytoday.com
Alabama Butterbean Festival	Early October	Pinson, Alabama, USA	www.butterbeanfestival.org
Navy Bean Festival	2nd week of October	Rising Sun, Indiana, USA	www.navybeanfestival.org
Feria de la Alubia Pinta Alavesa	2nd weekend in October	Pobes, Ribera Alta, Spain	www.alavaturismo.com
Concurso de Putxera (Puchera bean casserole competition)	Mid-October	San Severino, Balmaseda, Bizkaia, Spain	www.balmaseda.net
La Fiera dei Santi e La Cisrà (Chickpea Stew Festival)	2nd November	Dogliani, Piedmont, Italy	www.comune.dogliani.cn.it
Semana de la Alubia (Black Bean Week)	November	Tolosa, Spain	www.tourism.euskadi.net
Día de la Alubia de Gernika	1st Saturday in November	Gernika-Lumo, Bizkaia, Spain	www.gernika-lumo.net
Smolyan Bean Festival	Last Saturday in November	Smilyan, near Smolyan, Bulgaria	http://evros-smolyan.eu/node/385
Festa della Cicerchia	End of November	Serra De'Conti, Ancona, Italy	www.cicerchiadiserradeconti.it
Festival de la Alubia de Anguiano (Caparrones Red Bean Festival)	End of November	Anguiano, La Rioja, Spain	www.valvanera.com
Fasolatha (Bean Soup Festival)	St Nicholas Day (early December)	Florina, Macedonia, Greece	

Black bean burgers with mushrooms, ginger and walnuts

Fermented black beans – which aren't actually black beans at all, but rather soya beans/soybeans that have blackened as a result of the fermentation process – are often mashed and used as a condiment in Chinese cooking. They are usually purchased in cans from Chinese supermarkets, and should be well rinsed before use as they are very salty. An alternative seasoning is soy sauce.

sunflower oil, for cooking
5 spring onions/scallions, trimmed and chopped
125 g/a generous cup chestnut mushrooms, trimmed and chopped
2 garlic cloves, finely chopped
2 teaspoons finely chopped fresh ginger
60 g/½ cup walnuts, chopped
1 tablespoon soy sauce or Chinese fermented black beans, rinsed and mashed
250 g/1¼ cups cooked, soaked dried black beans, or the contents of 1 x 400-g/14-oz. can, drained
30 g/¼ cup rice flour
½ cucumber, thinly sliced, to serve
a small bunch of spring onions/scallions, trimmed and sliced, to serve
sweet pickled ginger, to serve

Makes 6.

The burgers can be fried or baked in the oven – if using the oven, preheat it to 180°C (350°F) Gas 4.

Hear 2 tablespoons of oil in a frying pan/skillet over a medium heat and fry the spring onions/ scallions, mushrooms, garlic and ginger for about 10 minutes, until the mushrooms have thrown off their liquid. Stir in the chopped walnuts and the soy sauce or mashed fermented beans.

Purée or mash half of the unfermented black beans and mix with the rice flour, then stir into the other ingredients and add the whole beans. Stir well.

Divide the mixture into 6 and, using 2 spoons, form 6 balls, then flatten them out to form burgers.

Brush a baking sheet with a little more oil, and heat in the oven. Place the burgers on the sheet, brush with a little more oil and bake for 20–30 minutes, turning them over during cooking. Alternatively, they can be fried.

Serve the burgers with a salad of sliced cucumber, spring onions/ scallions and some sweet pickled ginger.

Spiced chickpea and spinach pasties

These little turnover pasties make ideal food for nibbling with drinks, or for taking on picnics. The filling is Middle Eastern in character, while the soft pastry dough is more likely to be found in the Republic of Georgia.

For the pastry:

175 g/⅓ cup plain/all-purpose flour
½ teaspoon salt
75 g/5 tablespoons butter, chilled and diced
2 eggs, beaten separately
5 tablespoons sour cream
1 tablespoon sesame seeds

For the filling:

250 g/1¼ cups cooked, soaked dried chickpeas (garbanzos), or the contents of 1 x 400-g/14-oz. can, drained
2 tablespoons tahini
1 teaspoon ground cumin
1 teaspoon ground coriander
200 g/7 oz. fresh spinach, cooked, squeezed dry and chopped
1 tablespoon freshly squeezed lemon juice
3 tablespoons olive oil
1 tablespoon chopped fresh flat-leaf parsley
2 tablespoons chopped fresh mint
1 tablespoon za'tar (Middle Eastern spice mixture), or 1 tablespoon mixed dried oregano and thyme
1 teaspoon salt
ground black pepper

Makes about 20

To make the pastry, sift the flour and salt into a bowl and, using your fingers, rub in the diced butter until the mixture resembles fine breadcrumbs. Or, put the flour, salt and butter into a food processor and pulse for a few seconds. Add one of the beaten eggs and the sour cream and continue to mix until the dough starts to form a ball, then stop immediately.

Wrap the dough in clingfilm/plastic wrap and chill in the fridge for 20 minutes, or until needed.

Meanwhile, make the filling. In the food processor, pulse the chickpeas to a rough purée, together with the tahini and the ground spices. Stir (but don't purée) in the chopped spinach, lemon juice, olive oil, fresh herbs and za'tar or dried herbs, then season with the salt and some pepper.

Preheat the oven to 200°C (400°F) Gas 6.

On a floured board, roll out the pastry thinly and cut circles about 9 cm/3½ in. in diameter. Place a spoonful of the chickpea mixture on each circle, brush the perimeter with some of the other beaten egg and fold over to make a little pasty. Place on a greased baking sheet, then repeat until all of the pastry has been used. Brush the surface of each pasty with more beaten egg, sprinkle with the sesame seeds and bake in the preheated oven for 15–20 minutes, until golden brown.

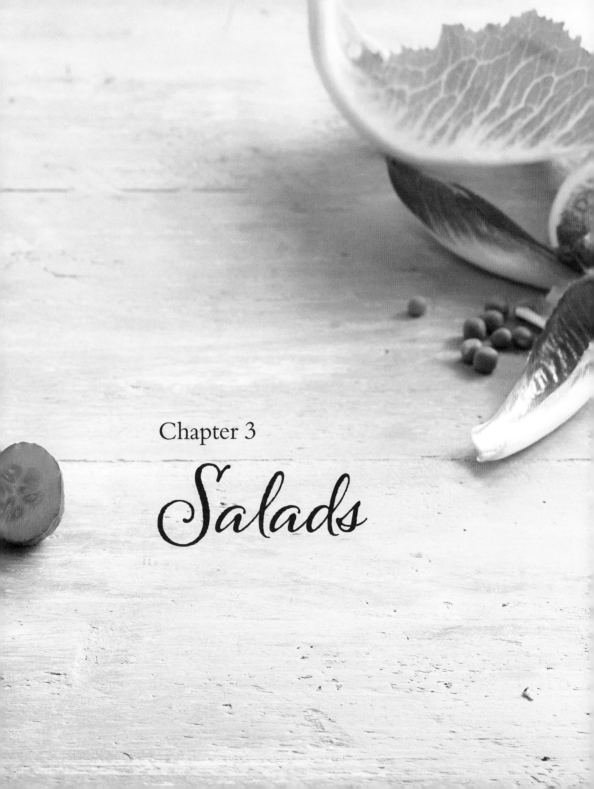

Chapter 3

Salads

Georgian red bean salad with walnuts and pomegranate seeds

Red beans, walnuts and pomegranates are a familiar sight in the markets of Georgia, a fascinating country at the crossroads of Europe and Asia. The visual contrast of deep red beans, sparkling pomegranate seeds and bright green herbs make this a handsome salad for autumn/fall.

2 tablespoons walnut, olive or sunflower oil

1 tablespoon pomegranate molasses

250 g/1¼ cups cooked, soaked dried red kidney beans, or the contents of 1 x 400-g/14-oz. can, drained

50 g/⅓ cup shelled walnuts

1 garlic clove, peeled, but left whole

1 tablespoon white wine vinegar

a small bunch of fresh flat-leaf parsley, coriander/cilantro and mint leaves, roughly chopped

½ teaspoon ground coriander

½ teaspoon ground cinnamon

a pinch of ground cloves

1 pomegranate

salt

½ teaspoon ground black pepper or cayenne pepper

Serves 4

Whisk together the oil and pomegranate molasses to make a dressing. Warm the beans in their cooking or canning liquid, then drain and toss them around in the dressing.

Grind or chop half of the walnuts and the garlic clove fairly finely – be careful not to reduce to a sticky paste if using an electric grinder – and mix in the vinegar. Add this, together with the chopped herbs and spices, to the beans and stir well to distribute all of the ingredients evenly. Season to taste with salt and the black or cayenne pepper.

Toast the remaining walnuts for a couple of minutes in a dry frying pan/skillet, then allow to cool and chop roughly.

Next, remove the seeds from the pomegranate. The easiest way to do this is to cut the fruit into quarters, roll back the segments to expose the seeds, then push the seeds into a bowl, picking out any bits of membrane as you go.

Mix the pomegranate seeds into the salad, strew the toasted chopped walnuts over and serve.

Salad of flageolet beans and fennel

This is a salad of contrasts: soft yet crunchy, sweet yet salty, and green and red.

250 g/1⅓ cups cooked, soaked dried flageolet beans, or the contents of 1 x 400-g/14-oz. can, drained
2 small or 1 large fennel bulb
2 tablespoons chopped fresh flat-leaf parsley or mint
1 thick slice of bread
2 tablespoons olive oil
6 slices of air-cured ham, such as prosciutto or 150 g/5 oz. mild goat's cheese
1 head of red chicory
1 crisp green apple
a few frilly lettuce leaves, to garnish
a small bunch of fresh chives, chopped/snipped, to garnish
salt and ground black pepper

For the vinaigrette:

1 teaspoon French mustard
2 tablespoons white wine vinegar
3 tablespoons olive oil
1 teaspoon toasted and crushed fennel seeds
1 tablespoon crème fraîche or sour cream
salt and ground black pepper

Serves 4-6

First make the vinaigrette by whisking the mustard into the vinegar, then adding all of the other ingredients and whisking these in vigorously until you have a creamy sauce. Season with salt and pepper.

Drain the cooked beans and mix them into the vinaigrette, or if using canned beans, rinse them with boiling water to get rid of the viscous liquid, then drain and mix into the vinaigrette. Warm beans will absorb the vinaigrette better than cold ones.

Trim the fennel bulbs then slice thinly and blend with the beans. Stir in the parsley or mint and set aside.

Cut the bread into 1 cm/⅜ in. cubes, and fry in the olive oil until crisp and brown. Lay them over a paper towel to drain off the excess oil.

Cut the goat's cheese into cubes, if using.

When ready to serve, assemble the salad. Slice the chicory head lengthways and toss the leaves into the bean mixture. Core the apple, but leave the skin on, and slice into thin wedges, then toss these in the salad, too. Spoon the bean mixture into the centre of a serving bowl, and arrange slices of ham around the outside of the salad (or strew with the cubes of cheese, if using) and croutons over the surface. Decorate with the frilly lettuce leaves and chopped chives, and season as desired.

Mung bean salad with mango, coconut and cucumber

A refreshing salad, which is simplicity itself to make.

150 g/¾ cup whole mung beans
1 tablespoon grated creamed
    coconut
½ cucumber, peeled, deseeded
    and chopped
½ under-ripe mango, peeled
    and cubed
1 fresh green chilli/chile, finely
    chopped
1 tablespoon olive oil
1 teaspoon mustard seeds
grated zest and freshly squeezed
    juice of 1 lime or lemon,
    to taste
2 tablespoons chopped fresh
    coriander/cilantro
salt and ground black pepper

Serves 4

Rinse the mung beans. Bring a saucepan of water to the boil, add the beans and simmer for 20–25 minutes, until they are just cooked, but not breaking up. Drain and transfer to a bowl, then stir in the grated coconut, mixing well so that it melts. Leave to cool.

When the beans are cold, stir in the cucumber, mango and green chilli/chile.

Heat the oil in a small frying pan/skillet, add the mustard seeds, and when they splutter, take the pan off the heat and pour the contents over the mixed salad ingredients. Sprinkle with the lime or lemon zest and juice, stir in the chopped coriander/cilantro, season with salt and pepper and serve immediately.

Black bean salad with avocado and lime

The Aztecs were already eating guacamole at the time of the Spanish Conquest, and the winning combination of avocado, chilli/chile, tomato and coriander/cilantro leaves, laced with lime, now rivals houmus in its universal popularity. By chopping the avocado instead of mashing it, and stirring in some cooked black beans, you have a salad with a distinctly Mexican flavour which is equally irresistible.

250 g/1¼ cups cooked, soaked dried black beans, drained, or the contents of 1 x 400-g/ 14-oz. can, rinsed and drained
1 lime
3 tablespoons olive oil
2 green chillies/chiles, finely chopped
1 tablespoon chopped fresh coriander/cilantro
1 tablespoon chopped fresh mint
a pinch of sugar (optional)
2 ripe avocados, stoned/pitted, peeled and chopped
250 g/8 oz. cherry tomatoes, cut in half
2 spring onions/scallions, trimmed and finely chopped
salt and ground black pepper

Serves 4.

Grate the zest of the lime into a bowl, then squeeze the juice into the same bowl. Whisk in the olive oil until the dressing emulsifies. Season with salt and black pepper, and stir in the chilli/chile and chopped fresh herbs. Taste the dressing, and if it seems too sharp, add a little bit of sugar.

Put the beans, avocados, tomatoes and spring onions/scallions into a large bowl and pour the dressing over. Toss everything together until all of the ingredients are blended, and serve.

Grow your own beans

In late summer, French, Spanish and Italian market stalls display boxes of colourful shelling beans for eating fresh from the pod. With their vivid colours and intricate patterns of both pods and seeds, especially when freshly shelled, they make a very rewarding garden crop on aesthetic grounds alone. But the melt-in-the-mouth texture and tender skins of beans fresh from the pod are a revelation.

Some years ago, I started to experiment with growing shelling beans, with good results. An entry from my first year's garden diary reads 'Best success with Borlotto Tongue of Fire (Lingua di Fuoco) – most prolific – magenta-streaked pods, beans large and celadon green when young, turning pink and creamy splodged, grey when cooked. Very good texture, smooth and thin skin, very tasty'.

My garden is high up in the Brecon Beacons of Wales, a region not famed for its benign climate, and that year I also wrote in my diary:

'Weather very wet and cold all summer, only improved in September. Many seeds didn't germinate. Went away at time when should have been planting out (May–June), and again at harvest (October).'

Yet even despite the inauspicious conditions, borlotti beans grew successfully, as did several other shelling beans. These included Trail of Tears, the black bean chosen by the Native American Cherokee people, when in 1838 they were forced to leave their homelands to make way for European settlers.

Other varieties that thrived in my garden were George's climbing French bean, good for eating green as well as shelled, and the Bird's Egg bean, which looks just as pretty as you would imagine and cooks well too.

I have been growing runner beans, not just for eating the green pods but also for shelling. White-flowered varieties such as Czar and White Lady produce white beans and by mid-September, instead of putting the plants on the compost heap,

I was shelling the pods and harvesting the delicious beans inside. With their thin skins and smooth buttery texture, they would compete with any of the most prized varieties found in Spain and Italy.

Out of curiosity, I also planted a few butter/ lima beans, the seeds bought not from a seed merchant but from the local health food shop at a considerably lower price. They grew, vigorously, into beanstalks that seemed to be heading fast for the sky, but actually stopped at about 3.5 m/12 ft., climbing their way though a nearby greengage tree. From the start, the plants closely resembled the runner beans, germinating with the cotyledons remaining below ground, and producing the same cream-and-white flowers in great profusion. By mid-September the fattening pods, though shorter than the runner beans, contained 3–4 pale green seeds, fat like puffed-up pillows and measuring 3 cm/1¼ in. in length. These turned out to be even tastier than the Czar or White Lady, with a soft, mealy texture and a very distinctive taste reminiscent of mushrooms.

Other successes, both closely related to runner beans, have been the Italian Fagioli di Spagna, which was probably marginally even more delectable than the butter/lima beans, with a refined taste and silky smooth texture, and huge fat Greek Gigantes.

Seeds for Tarbais beans came from wholesalers in New Covent Garden Market, in South London. They supply them to the restaurant trade, where they are regarded as the beans of choice for cassoulet. Cooked straight from the pod, they are out of this world, with a completely smooth, silky texture and delicate, distinctly beany, flavour. The crop was scant, but that may have been due to the inclement weather.

Freshly podded beans only need cooking for a relatively short time – around 20 minutes. They hardly need any sauce or dressing – a *persillade* of

finely chopped parsley, garlic and butter is ideal – but plain butter or olive oil is fine too. They make a great addition to minestrone soup.

Sown in pots or root trainers in the greenhouse in early May, the seedlings can be planted out when they are about 10 cm/4 in. tall and all danger of frost is past. Climbing varieties need bamboo canes as a support, just like runner beans. Keep the plants moist, and pinch out the growing shoot when it reaches the top of the canes.

The beans can be eaten fresh, semi-dry or dry. Beans for drying and storing should be left on the vine to dry until the pods are brittle and the beans inside rattle when the pod is shaken. Then they are ready to pick, preferably on a dry day and definitely before the first frost. In bad weather, the whole plant can be uprooted and left to dry in an airy shed before shelling and storing the beans.

Recommended bush varieties for growing in the UK and parts of the US include Horsehead (maroon beans), Coquette (small white beans) and Brown Dutch (pale brown beans). Dwarf varieties of borlotti beans are more reliable in cool, wet summers as they crop earlier than climbers and can be protected with fleece if the weather turns cold. The Italian seed merchants Franchi Seeds have a good selection of borlotti beans including two dwarf varieties, Stregonta Nano and Borlotto di Vigevano, but any of the climbing borlotti should also produce a crop in a good growing season.

Other sources of unusual beans include Garden Organic's Heritage Seed Library, which cleverly gets round EU legislation preventing the sale of many rare varieties by giving their members free samples. Local seed swaps are another good way of finding these treasures. By growing these endangered varieties you will be helping to preserve something valuable that would otherwise disappear.

A word of warning – it is unwise to eat raw beans once they have formed sizeable seeds as they may contain the same toxins found in dried beans (see pages 13–14 for a fuller explanation).

Salad of Puy lentils with roasted beetroot

The habit of serving lentils with beet(root) goes back to Roman times. Writing in 2nd-century Rome, the physician and philosopher Galen recommended this health-giving combination in his treatise *On the Power of Foods*, dressing the salad with a sweet and salty fish sauce. If a fishy taste appeals, add some fish sauce to the dressing instead of salt. Serve the salad on its own, or strewn with crumbled salty cheese, such as feta, or slices of grilled halloumi cheese.

500 g/1 lb. beet(root), peeled and cut into wedges
3 tablespoons olive oil
3 fresh or dried bay leaves
1 sprig of fresh thyme or 1 teaspoon dried thyme
200 g/1 cup dried Puy or French green lentils, rinsed and drained
2 garlic cloves, peeled but left whole
3 tablespoons chopped fresh flat-leaf parsley
2 tablespoons chopped fresh mint
salt and ground black pepper

For the dressing

1 tablespoon balsamic vinegar
1 tablespoon maple syrup
2 tablespoons freshly squeezed lemon juice
2 tablespoons olive oil
salt and ground black pepper

Serves 4–6

Preheat the oven to 180°C (350°F) Gas 4.

Place the beet(root) in a small roasting pan, and toss in 2 tablespoons of the olive oil together with 3 tablespoons of water, 2 of the bay leaves and the thyme. Season with salt and pepper, cover with aluminium foil and roast in the preheated oven until they are soft – about 1 hour.

Meanwhile, boil the lentils in a saucepan of water, together with the whole garlic cloves and the remaining bay leaf and olive oil, for about 30 minutes, or until thoroughly cooked.

Whisk the ingredients for the dressing together.

Drain the lentils and stir in all but 1 tablespoon of the dressing and the chopped fresh herbs. Arrange the chunks of cooked beet(root) over, drizzle with the remaining dressing and serve at room temperature.

Salad of marinated chicken and black-eyed beans

Escabeche, or *escabetx* in Catalan, is an ancient Arabic method of preserving fish or meat, which is especially popular in the Latin world. Intended to be served cold, the preparation is both simple and quick, although it does have to be made 24 hours before serving, as the meat or fish must cool and marinate in the cooking liquid, soaking up its delicious flavours in the process. This is a reconstruction of a salad that I enjoyed in the Catalan city of Girona. It was made with an *escabetx* of partridge, but chicken makes a fine substitute if you can't find partridge.

125 ml/½ cup olive oil, plus 2 tablespoons for frying
60 ml/¼ cup red wine vinegar
6 garlic cloves, peeled but left whole
4 spring onions/scallions, trimmed
1 carrot, peeled and cut in half
2 fresh or dried bay leaves
3 branches of fresh thyme
1 teaspoon whole black peppercorns
2 leg-and-thigh joints of chicken or 2 whole partridges
1 tablespoon chopped fresh mint
250 g/1¼ cups cooked, soaked dried black-eyed beans/peas, or the contents of 1 x 400-g/14-oz. can, drained
2 tablespoons chopped fresh flat-leaf parsley
2 Little Gem or 1 small Cos/Romaine lettuce, washed

For the dressing

4 tablespoons olive oil
1 tablespoon red wine vinegar
½ teaspoon caster/granulated sugar
salt and ground black pepper

Serves 4

Heat the 2 tablespoons of olive oil in a large frying pan/skillet and fry the chicken joints or partridges gently, until brown all over, turning them over from time to time.

Add the rest of the oil, the vinegar, garlic, spring onions/scallions, carrot, bay leaves, thyme and peppercorns, and enough salted water to just cover everything, then cover the pan/skillet and bring to the boil.

Simmer very gently for about 1 hour, until the meat is beginning to fall off the bones. Take off the heat and leave in a cool place overnight.

The next day, use a colander to strain the contents of the pan into a large bowl. Put the stock in the fridge for 1–2 hours, then skim most of the fat from the surface. Reserve the jellified liquid. Remove the chicken or partridge, and pick the meat off the bones, discarding all of the skin and gristle. Cut the meat into bite-size pieces and moisten with a little of the jellified liquid, saving the rest for stock. Add the mint, season with salt and pepper and mix thoroughly. This is the escabeche.

Make a dressing for the salad with the oil, vinegar, sugar and seasoning, then use 1 tablespoon of this to dress the lettuce.

Toss the beans in the remaining dressing with the parsley.

Divide the lettuce between 4 serving plates, put a serving of beans followed by a serving of escabeche on top of each and serve at once.

Quinoa and butter bean salad with avocado

Based on a dish I enjoyed at a Peruvian restaurant in Soho, this satisfying salad has a pleasing combination of textures enlivened by the lime–chilli dressing.

125 g/½ cup quinoa
250 g/1¼ cups cooked, soaked dried butter/lima beans, or the contents of 1 x 400-g/14-oz. can, drained
½ red onion, very finely diced
1 ripe avocado, stoned/pitted, peeled and diced
2 tomatoes, finely chopped
2 tablespoons fresh coriander/ cilantro, roughly chopped, to serve

For the vinaigrette:
4 tablespoons olive oil
2 tablespoons freshly squeezed lime juice
1 (or more) fresh green chillies/chiles, deseeded and finely chopped
1 teaspoon sugar
salt and ground black pepper

Serves 4–6

Wash the quinoa thoroughly, place in a saucepan and add 375 ml/1½ cups of cold water. Cover the pan and bring to the boil, then simmer for 20 minutes, by which time the water should have been absorbed. Take off the heat, fluff up the grains with a fork and leave to cool.

Combine the butter/lima beans, red onion, avocado and tomatoes in a large bowl. Stir in the cooked quinoa.

Make the vinaigrette by either whisking all the ingredients together in a bowl with a fork or a balloon whisk, or by whizzing them up in a small blender.

Stir the dressing into the bowl containing all of the other ingredients, add the chopped coriander/cilantro and serve.

Chickpea, egg and potato salad

A pleasing combination of flavours and textures, the nutty chickpeas are bound together by the slightly broken-up potato, hard-boiled egg and oily dressing. This has been a family favourite for as long as I can remember. It tastes best when it's still warm.

250 g/1¼ cups cooked, soaked dried chickpeas, or the contents of 1 x 400-g/14-oz. can, drained
500 g/1 lb. salad potatoes, boiled and bashed gently
a handful of olives, green or black
3 hard-boiled/cooked eggs, peeled and roughly chopped
a handful of fresh chives, chopped/snipped

For the vinaigrette:
4 tablespoons olive oil
1 tablespoon white wine vinegar
1 tablespoon chopped fresh flat-leaf parsley
1 garlic clove, crushed
salt and ground black pepper

Serves 4

Make the vinaigrette by whisking all the ingredients together in a bowl with a fork or a balloon whisk. Set aside.

Mash one-third of the chickpeas slightly, then mix them with the whole chickpeas and the potatoes. Add the olives and vinaigrette and stir well.

Distribute the chopped eggs through the salad, taking care not to break them up too much. Sprinkle the chives over the surface and serve immediately.

Chapter 4

Main Dishes

Valencian paella

Contrary to popular belief, paella originally consisted of rice, beans and snails, with the occasional addition of water vole or eel if available. On high days and holidays, rabbit or chicken would be added to the paella, but although there are now many versions of the dish, the true Valencian paella does not include shellfish. It is a simple dish with few ingredients, in total contrast to more familiar 'luxury' versions that can be found in yachting marinas the world over. The beans would have been a mixture of what was available, for example, flat green beans rather like runner beans, white beans resembling cannellini and known as *mongetes* in Catalan, and *garrafones* – fresh butter/lima beans.

½ teaspoon saffron strands
2 tablespoons olive oil
750 g/1½ lbs. chicken
   or rabbit joints
1 onion, finely chopped
4 tomatoes, halved and grated
250 g/8 oz. runner beans, sliced
250 g/1¼ cups cooked, soaked
   dried cannellini or butter/lima
   beans, or the contents of
   1 x 400-g/14-oz. can, drained
900 ml/3¾ cups chicken stock
1 tablespoon chopped fresh
   rosemary
250 g/1¼ cups short-grain rice,
   such as Bomba
salt and ground black pepper

Serves 4

Put the saffron in a small bowl and pour 2 tablespoons of boiling water over it, then leave to soak for 30 minutes.

Heat the oil in a wide shallow frying pan/skillet and sauté the chicken or rabbit pieces until golden brown, then remove and set aside. Keep the chicken or rabbit warm while you prepare the vegetables.

In the same pan/skillet, gently fry the onion until soft and translucent, then add the grated tomatoes and the saffron with its water, and continue to cook for a further 5 minutes.

Put the chicken or rabbit back into the pan/skillet with the onion and tomato and add the stock and rosemary. Bring to the boil, then simmer for about 10 minutes, uncovered. Taste the stock and season with salt and pepper.

Next, add the rice and prepared beans, distributing them evenly and pushing them them down so that they are submerged in the stock, and continue to cook, uncovered, for about 25–30 minutes, or until the rice and beans are cooked and the liquid has been absorbed. During this final cooking, leave the dish well alone.

If it seems to be drying out before the rice is cooked, add a little boiling water or extra stock, but don't stir it in.

Once cooked, it will sit quite happily for quite a while, covered with a lid or clean, damp cloth/rag. In any case, it should be allowed to sit for a few minutes before serving – in Spain it is normal to eat paella tepid rather than hot.

Seared squid with white beans and fennel

Seafood and beans have a special affinity that is often overlooked, and this is an example of that happy combination.

1 onion, sliced
3 tablespoons olive oil
3 garlic cloves, finely chopped
1 fennel bulb, trimmed, halved and thinly sliced crossways
1 teaspoon fennel seeds, lightly crushed
100 ml/6 tablespoons white wine
3 large tomatoes
250 g/1¼ cups cooked, soaked dried white beans, such as cannellini or the contents of 2 x 400-g/14-oz. cans, drained
500 g/1 lb. fresh squid, cleaned
1 lemon, cut into wedges, for squeezing
salt and ground black pepper

For the parsley oil

3 tablespoons very finely chopped fresh flat-leaf parsley
75 ml/5 tablespoons olive oil
salt and ground black pepper

Serves 4

Whisk together the ingredients for the parsley oil in a bowl with a fork or balloon whisk, whisking in a little water to loosen the mixture, then set aside.

In a frying pan/skillet, fry the onion in 2 tablespoons of the olive oil for about 5 minutes, then add the garlic and sliced fennel, together with the fennel seeds. Continue to sauté gently for another 10–15 minutes, until the vegetables are soft, then add the wine and cook for another few minutes, until half of the liquid has evaporated. Cut the tomatoes in half, and grate the flesh into the pan/skillet, discarding the skin.

Mix the cooked beans with the fennel and tomato. Season with salt and pepper and keep the mixture warm while you cook the squid.

Remove the membrane from the squid, make sure it is thoroughly clean by rinsing under running water, then pat dry with paper towels. Cut the body in half and lay it flat, skin-side up, on a chopping board. Using a sharp knife, score a lattice pattern on the surface, taking care not to cut right through, then cut the squid into 3.5-cm/1½-in. square pieces, and toss the pieces around in a bowl with the remaining oil so that each piece is well coated.

Heat a non-stick frying pan/skillet. When it is really hot, brush the pan/skillet with oil and sear the squid for 1 minute on each side, until lightly browned, then remove from the pan/skillet.

Place a spoonful of the bean mixture onto each plate, and a portion of squid on top. Drizzle some of the parsley oil over and squeeze a little lemon juice over the top.

White beans with clams

The Spanish province of Asturias is best known for its *Fabada Asturiana*, a savoury stew of white beans with chorizo, black pudding and ham. However, this Asturian bean dish – known locally as *Fabes con almejas* – looks to the sea for its inspiration. Ideally it should be made with genuine *fabes asturianas*, the prized white beans with thin skins and silken smooth flesh that are protected by the denomination of origin certification. They can be bought from specialist suppliers of Spanish food, but are otherwise hard to come by.

30 saffron strands
500 g/2¾ cups dried white beans, such as *fabes asturianas*, cannellini or butter/lima beans, soaked overnight and drained
1 onion, chopped
3 garlic cloves, chopped
1 carrot, peeled and chopped
a small bunch of fresh flat-leaf parsley, tied together with string
3 tablespoons olive oil
2 fresh or dried bay leaves
24 live clams, soaked in salt water for a few hours
2 tablespoons white wine
1 tablespoon sweet paprika or pimentón (optional)
salt and ground black pepper
crusty bread, to serve

Serves 4–6

Crumble the saffron into a small bowl, and pour 1 tablespoon of hot water over it, then leave to infuse while you prepare the rest of the ingredients.

Place the beans, onion, garlic, carrot, parsley, bay leaves and olive oil in a large saucepan, then add enough water to cover everything and bring to the boil. After boiling briskly for 10 minutes, turn the heat down very low, cover the pan and cook for 1½–3 hours, until the beans are soft. During this time, shake the pan every so often, but don't stir the contents or the beans will break up. If necessary, add extra hot water, just to cover the beans but taking care not to drown them.

Towards the end of the cooking time, drain the clams and place in a separate saucepan with the white wine and cook over a medium heat, with the lid on, until all of the clams have opened. This will only take a few minutes – lift the lid to inspect every minute or so and take off the heat as soon as they have all opened. Discard any that refuse to open.

Add the saffron and its golden liquid to the pan of beans and remove the bunch of parsley and the bay leaves. Stir in the sweet paprika or pimentón, if using. Using tongs, transfer the clams to the pan of beans, then strain the cooking liquid into the pan, using a fine sieve/strainer or muslin/cheesecloth to remove any grit.

Shake the pan gently from side to side, to amalgamate all of the juices without breaking up the beans. Simmer everything together gently for a few minutes to blend in the flavours. Add salt and pepper to taste.

Spoon the beans into shallow soup bowls, place 6 clams on each and serve with crusty bread, and a glass of dry cider, as they do in Asturias.

Catalan rice with chickpeas, smoked haddock and red pepper

Based on a Lenten recipe from Spain, where salt cod would be used, this makes use of smoked haddock in place of cod.

300 g/10 oz. undyed smoked haddock fillet

250 g/1¼ cups cooked, soaked dried chickpeas (garbanzos) or the contents of 1 x 400-g/14-oz. can, drained

a generous pinch of saffron strands

1 red (bell) pepper

2 large tomatoes

3 tablespoons olive oil

6 garlic cloves, finely chopped

250 g/1¼ cups short-grain rice, such as Bomba

2 hard-boiled/cooked eggs, peeled and cut into quarters

Serves 4

Poach the smoked haddock gently in water for about 5 minutes, until it flakes easily, and then drain. Flake the fish with a fork, removing any stray bones and skin, and set aside.

Warm the chickpeas in a little water, crumbling the strands of saffron lightly with your fingers into the pan. Simmer very gently for about 20 minutes, during which time they will take on the colour and flavour of the saffron. Drain through a sieve/strainer, reserving the golden cooking water, and set both aside.

Cut the red (bell) pepper in half lengthways, remove the stalk and seeds and put the 2 halves under the grill, skin-side up, until the skins blacken. Put the pepper into a plastic bag for a few minutes, then lift off the blackened skins and slice the 2 halves into thin strips.

Either blanch the tomatoes in boiling water for 1 minute, peel, deseed and chop the pulp, or cut in half crossways, scrape out the seeds and grate the cut side of each half into a shallow bowl, leaving the skin behind. This is the Catalan way of doing it; they even grow special varieties of tomato for grating, with tough skins.

Heat the olive oil in a pan and cook the garlic gently for 1–2 minutes, until it becomes golden and ceases to smell of raw garlic. Be careful not to burn it. Add the tomato pulp and cook for another 5 minutes or so, until it has disintegrated, and then tip the rice into the pan and stir around thoroughly until every grain is coated. Add 600 ml/2½ cups of water, including the saffron-flavoured chickpeas' cooking water, and bring to the boil. Simmer for 20 minutes, uncovered, until the rice is cooked and no liquid remains. Adjust the seasoning, bearing in mind that the smoked fish is already quite salty.

Stir in the chickpeas and flaked fish, heat through for a few minutes, then strew the strips of red (bell) pepper over. Place the hard-boiled egg quarters on top of everything. Keep in a warm place for 10 minutes for the flavours to meld together, then serve.

Cassoulet

Before white beans arrived in Europe after the discovery of the Americas, cassoulet was probably made with dried broad/fava beans and maybe a few bacon rinds for flavouring, but over the years this rustic hotpot from south-west France has become ever more elaborate.

For the bean mixture:

400 g/2 cups dried white beans (Tarbais, Soissons or cannellini), soaked overnight
1 onion, peeled but left whole
a bouquet garni, comprising a branch of fresh thyme, a fresh or dried bay leaf and a small bunch of fresh flat-leaf parsley, tied together with string
2 garlic cloves, peeled but left whole
1 carrot, peeled and sliced in half
100 g/3½ oz. pork rind (from the pork belly, see below)
5 black peppercorns

For the meat:

2 confit duck leg and thigh joints or 2 fresh duck legs (approximately 500 g/1 lb.)
350 g/12 oz. pork belly or shoulder, rind and excess fat removed, meat cut into cubes
30 g/2 tablespoons goose or duck fat
350 g/12 oz. Toulouse sausages, or other coarse sausages with a high meat content
150 g/5 oz. smoked bacon lardons
1 onion, chopped
4 garlic cloves, chopped
1 tablespoon tomato purée/paste
4 tablespoons fresh breadcrumbs
salt and ground black pepper

Serves 4–5

Drain the beans, and add to a large saucepan with enough fresh water to cover them. Boil for 10 minutes, drain and put back in the pan together with the other ingredients for the bean cooking. Cover with fresh water and bring to the boil, then cover the pan, reduce the heat and simmer very gently for 40 minutes.

Preheat the oven to 150°C (300°F) Gas 2.

While the beans are cooking, warm the confit duck or fresh duck leg joints in a frying pan/skillet until the fat and juices run. Remove the duck and set aside, then scrape the fat and pan juices into a small jug/pitcher and leave to cool. Skim the fat off the surface and use this to fry the meats in the same frying pan/skillet. Set aside the juices for later.

In the same pan/skillet, fry the pork belly in the goose or duck fat until nicely browned (you may need extra fat). Remove the pork and fry the sausages until brown, then remove them and fry the bacon, onion and garlic for a few minutes until starting to brown. Mix the pork with the bacon and onion mixture.

Drain the beans, retaining the cooking liquid, and discard the pork rind, onion, carrot and bouquet garni. Mash the garlic cloves with a fork.

Put half of the beans into the bottom of a large ovenproof casserole dish, cover with half of the pork mixture, then add the rest of the beans followed by the remaining meat, placing the sausages and duck legs on top, skin-side up.

Stir the tomato purée/paste and the set-aside cooking juices into the bean cooking liquid, then pour just enough into the casserole to cover the beans. Cover and cook in the oven for about 1½ hours.

Take the casserole out and remove the duck legs. Take the meat off the bone and cut into chunks, then return these to the pot. Give everything a good stir, taste and add seasoning if necessary.

Sprinkle the breadcrumbs over the surface of the cassoulet, then put the dish back in the oven, uncovered, for another hour or until the top is crisp and brown.

Serve immediately with some good bread and green salad to follow.

Hungarian red bean hotpot with smoked ham and barley

Solet is the Hungarian version of *cholent*, the hearty bean casserole traditionally prepared on Friday in Jewish households to be cooked very slowly overnight for consumption on the Sabbath. It is a rich, comforting dish for autumn/fall or winter. There are as many recipes for *solet* as there are Hungarian mothers, and today many, such as this one, include non-kosher ingredients.

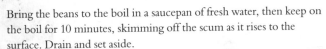

400 g/2¼ cups dried red beans, soaked in water for 12 hours and drained
2 onions, finely chopped
30 g/2 tablespoons goose or duck fat, or sunflower oil
2 duck leg and thigh joints (about 500 g/1 lb. in total)
2 teaspoons smoked paprika/pimentón or sweet Hungarian paprika
150 g/¾ cup dried pearl barley, rinsed and drained
1 spiced sausage, kolbász or chorizo, about 200 g/6½ oz.
about 500 g/1 lb. smoked gammon or 1 ham hock (about 500 g/1 lb.), preferably smoked
6 eggs (optional)
salt and ground black pepper
dill-pickled cucumbers, to serve

Serves 8

Bring the beans to the boil in a saucepan of fresh water, then keep on the boil for 10 minutes, skimming off the scum as it rises to the surface. Drain and set aside.

In a large ovenproof cast-iron casserole dish, sauté the onions in the fat or oil, then add the duck legs and brown lightly. Remove the duck and set aside, turn the heat down very low and sprinkle the smoked or sweet paprika over the onions, stirring it constantly and making sure it doesn't scorch, which it does very easily. Cook very briefly, then tip the beans into the dish, stirring them into the onions. Add the barley and stir again. Make a hollow on the top of the beans and sit the piece of smoked gammon or ham hock in the hollow. Arrange the sausage and duck legs, skin-side up, around the ham and pour in enough water to cover the beans by 3 cm/1¼ in. Bring gently to the boil.

Meanwhile, preheat the oven to 140°C (275°F) Gas 1. Cover the casserole with a tight-fitting lid and place it in the preheated oven.

After 4 hours, take the casserole dish out of the oven. Remove the skin, gristle and bones from the various types of meat, divide into bite-sized chunks and stir back into the beans.

Wash the eggs thoroughly and place them, in their shells, around the outside of the dish, pushed down into the bean mixture. If necessary, add a little more water, then continue the cooking for another hour or so, until the beans are soft and most of the liquid has been absorbed by the beans and barley. The finished dish should not be dry, but neither should it be mushy.

Season with salt and pepper. Peel the eggs, cut them in half and place them, cut-side up, around the outside of the casserole dish. For an authentic Hungarian touch, serve with dill-pickled cucumbers.

Chicken k'dra with chickpeas and saffron

This aromatic Moroccan chicken stew, or *k'dra*, resembles a tagine in many ways, but for the use of butter or *smen* instead of oil as the cooking medium. *Smen* is similar to clarified butter, made by boiling butter until the milk solids can be separated out by skimming and then straining through muslin/cheesecloth. It can be stored in the fridge for some time, and if used within a few weeks, tastes pleasantly nutty. Berbers favour storing their *smen* for up to a year, as they like the rancid flavour it acquires, but nowadays town people in Morocco use fresh butter instead. The traditional way of cooking this *k'dra* is to simmer soaked chickpeas together with the chicken, but unless you are sure that they are fresh enough to cook within the hour, you risk overcooking the chicken.

30 g/2 tablespoons butter
1 chicken (approximately 1.4 kg/3 lbs.), jointed into 8 pieces, or 8 chicken thighs, excess fat removed
1 cinnamon stick
2 teaspoons ground ginger
100 g/3½ oz. whole blanched almonds
3 large onions, finely sliced
a generous pinch of saffron, soaked in 2 tablespoons of hot water for 5 minutes
300 ml/1¼ cups chicken stock or water
250 g/1¼ cups cooked, soaked dried chickpeas (garbanzos), or the contents of 1 x 400-g/14-oz. can, drained
a bunch of fresh flat-leaf parsley, chopped
freshly squeezed juice of ½ lemon
salt and ground black pepper
steamed couscous, to serve

Melt the butter in a large, lidded casserole dish or frying pan/skillet. Add the chicken pieces, together with the cinnamon, ginger and whole almonds, turning everything around to coat it all in butter. Cook gently for about 10 minutes, uncovered.

Add 2 of the sliced onions and stir into the buttery mixture, then add the saffron with its soaking water and the stock or water. Cover the casserole dish or frying pan/skillet and simmer for about 30 minutes.

Add the chickpeas and the third onion and stir in the chopped parsley, then bring back to the boil and simmer, covered, for another 30 minutes, or until the chicken is very tender.

Remove the chicken pieces and keep warm. If necessary, reduce the sauce by simmering it uncovered for about 15 minutes in order to thicken it and concentrate the flavour. Season with salt and pepper, add the lemon juice and return the chicken to the pot.

Serve with steamed couscous.

Serves 4

Pot-roast guinea fowl with Puy lentils

Guinea fowl has more flavour than chicken, but can be on the dry side. In this recipe, moisture from the vegetables prevents the bird drying out, and all of the delectable cooking juices are stirred into the lentils at the end, together with cream and balsamic vinegar as a final enrichment.

1 tablespoon olive oil
1 guinea fowl (approximately 1.3 kg/2¾ lbs.)
2 teaspoons butter
1 onion, chopped
2 garlic cloves, chopped
1 carrot, peeled and diced
1 celery stick/rib, diced
2 fresh or dried bay leaves
1 sprig of fresh thyme
200 ml/¾ cup chicken stock or water
75 ml/⅓ cup Marsala or Amontillado Sherry
125 g/a generous ½ cup Puy/French green lentils
1 tablespoon balsamic vinegar
2 tablespoons double/heavy cream
salt and ground black pepper

Serves 2–4

Preheat the oven to 180°C (350°F) Gas 4.

Heat the olive oil in an ovenproof cast-iron casserole dish and brown the guinea fowl on all sides. If you haven't got a casserole dish, use a frying pan/skillet to brown the bird, and then transfer it to an ovenproof baking dish. Keep it warm while you cook the vegetables.

If you have an ovenproof cast-iron casserole dish, add the butter to it and soften the chopped onion and garlic, then add the carrot and celery and cook for another 5 minutes. If you're using a frying pan/skillet, follow the same instructions, but transfer the vegetables to the ovenproof baking dish containing the browned guinea fowl.

Put the guinea fowl on its side on top of the vegetables, push one of the bay leaves and the thyme beneath the surface of the vegetables and pour over the stock and Marsala or Sherry. Cover the dish with a lid or kitchen foil and roast in the oven for 45 minutes, turning the bird over halfway through cooking.

Meanwhile, rinse and drain the lentils, then place in a pan of cold water with the remaining bay leaf. Bring to the boil, then simmer for about 20 minutes. Drain and keep warm.

When the guinea fowl has been cooking for 45 minutes, uncover it, turn onto its back and brown in the oven for another 20 minutes. Make sure the bird is cooked by sticking a skewer between the thigh and the breast and checking that the juices are running clear.

Take the guinea fowl out of the dish and joint it by removing first the legs and thighs, then the breasts, which can be cut in half. Keep warm while you stir the lentils, balsamic vinegar, cream and seasoning into the vegetables. Lay the pieces of guinea fowl on top of the lentils and serve immediately.

Persian lamb casserole with chickpeas and herbs

Rich lamb stews are very popular in Iran, although traditionally they would often contain very little meat. All kinds of vegetables, fruits and pulses would be added to give body to the hotpot, as well as handfuls of fresh herbs, and the stew is usually served with rice. Iranians love the sweet and sour flavours that were a feature of many medieval English dishes, a formula that survives to this day in the form of the traditional mint sauce which accompanies roast lamb.

3 tablespoons olive oil

1 kg/2 lbs. shoulder of lamb, bone, fat and gristle removed, cubed

3 large onions, chopped

8 garlic cloves, chopped finely

2 teaspoons ground cinnamon

2 teaspoons ground turmeric

500 g/2½ cups cooked, soaked dried chickpeas (garbanzos), or the contents of 2 x 400-g/14-oz. cans, drained

6 tomatoes, skinned and chopped

3 tablespoons white wine, freshly squeezed lime juice or verjuice

200 g/7 oz. spinach or Swiss chard leaves, chopped

a generous handful of chopped fresh coriander/cilantro and mint

salt and ground black pepper

sugar, to taste

pomegranate seeds or barberries, if available, to serve

boiled rice, to serve

Greek yogurt, to serve

warmed flatbread, to serve

Serves 6

Heat 2 tablespoons of olive oil in a large casserole dish or frying pan/skillet and fry the lamb until browned. You may have to do this half at a time to ensure that the meat is nicely caramelized on the surface. Add the onions and garlic to the pan and cook gently until soft. Then add the spices, chickpeas, tomatoes and wine, lime juice or verjuice. Stir well, adding a splash or water if necessary, cover and simmer for around 1 hour, until the lamb is tender.

Towards the end of cooking, sauté the spinach or chard leaves in a tablespoon of olive oil, and add to the casserole. Stir in the chopped fresh herbs.

If using barberries, soak them in water for 10 minutes, then sauté briefly in oil.

Check the seasoning, adding salt, pepper and sugar to taste. Strew pomegranate seeds or barberries over and serve with boiled rice, Greek yogurt and warmed flatbread.

Lamb dhansak with squash and lentils

A speciality of the Parsi sect that combines elements of Persian cookery with that of Gujarat in western India, this hot, sweet and sour lamb stew can contain as many as nine different kinds of pulse, as well as a variety of vegetables, all simmered with garlic, chillies/chiles, cinnamon and turmeric.

For the lentil mixture:

2 tablespoons vegetable oil

1 onion, chopped

75 g/⅓ cup dried pigeon peas (toor dal)

75 g/⅓ cup dried red lentils (masoor dal)

75 g/⅓ cup dried black gram (urid beans)

1 aubergine/eggplant, chopped

1 small sweet potato, or 250 g/8 oz. squash, peeled, deseeded and chopped

1 teaspoon ground turmeric

3 fresh green chillies/chiles, deseeded and finely chopped

250 g/1¼ cups cooked, soaked dried chickpeas (garbanzos), or the contents of 1 x 400-g/ 14-oz. can, drained

For the spice mixture:

1 teaspoon cumin seeds

3 teaspoons coriander seeds

1 teaspoon fenugreek seeds

5 black peppercorns

5 cardamom seeds

For the lamb mixture:

2 tablespoons vegetable oil or ghee

2 onions, finely chopped

6 garlic cloves, finely chopped

2.5-cm/1-in. cube of fresh ginger, peeled and grated

2 dried red chillies/chiles

½ cinnamon stick

500 g/1 lb. boneless lamb, cubed

2 tomatoes, skinned and chopped, or ½ x 400-g/14-oz. can chopped tomatoes

freshly squeezed juice of 1 lime

a bunch of fresh coriander/cilantro, chopped

2 tablespoons torn fresh mint leaves

salt

boiled rice, to serve

Serves 4

Rinse and drain all the lentils. Heat the oil in a medium-sized pan/skillet and fry the onion until soft. Add the lentils and all of the other ingredients for the lentil mixture, just cover with water and bring to the boil. Cover the pan/skillet, turn down the heat and simmer for about 40 minutes, until all of the ingredients are very soft. You may need to add more hot water during cooking. Mash half of the mixture with a potato masher or wooden spoon, return to the pan/skillet and set aside.

While the lentil mixture is cooking, dry roast the cumin, coriander and fenugreek seeds together with the peppercorns, then grind them with the cardamom in a coffee grinder or food chopper.

For the lamb mixture, heat the oil or ghee in a frying pan/skillet large enough to take all of the ingredients, and gently fry the onions until brown. Add the garlic, ginger, chillies/chiles and cinnamon and fry for another few minutes. Tip in the spice mixture and cook for another 5 minutes, stirring constantly to prevent the mixture sticking to the bottom of the pan/skillet. Add the lamb and stir around to coat the meat in the spice mixture and to brown the surface of the meat.

Add the tomatoes and a little water (or stock) and bring to the boil. Cover the pan/skillet, turn down the heat and simmer very gently for about 1 hour, or until the meat is tender. Stir in the cooked lentils and vegetables. Add the lime juice, coriander/ cilantro and mint, then season with salt and heat through thoroughly.

Serve with boiled rice.

Mutton stew with maple peas and mint

Maple peas, or Black Badgers as they are sometimes called, had all but disappeared until recently but are now enjoying something of a revival and can be bought in health food shops or direct from a company called Hodmedods. Traditionally eaten in Lancashire, in the north-west of England, especially at fun fairs around Bonfire Night (5th November), they were also sold at other times of year by street vendors in Preston and Bolton, like sweet chestnuts or baked potatoes. In Yorkshire they are eaten on Carling Sunday, the fifth Sunday in Lent, and are known as Carlin peas. They have a lovely taste all of their own, reminiscent of chestnuts. The Lancashire way to eat maple peas is with salt and vinegar, so I've carried on this tradition by adding them to a rich mutton stew.

750 g/1⅔ lbs. boneless lean shoulder of mutton or stewing lamb
1 tablespoon plain/all-purpose flour
2 tablespoons olive oil
2 large onions, sliced
1 large carrot, peeled and sliced
500 ml/2 cups lamb or vegetable stock
2 fresh or dried bay leaves
1 tablespoon chopped fresh rosemary leaves
175 g/1 scant cup dried maple peas, soaked overnight in water or the contents of 1½ x 400-g/14-oz. cans, drained
1 tablespoon balsamic vinegar
2 tablepoons chopped fresh mint
salt and ground black pepper
buttery, crusty bread, to serve

Serves 4-6

Preheat the oven to 120°C (250°F) Gas ½.

Cut the meat into chunks and heat the oil. An ovenproof cast-iron casserole dish is ideal for this, as it can go straight into the oven, but the initial frying can be done in a frying pan/skillet before transferring the meat and onions to an ovenproof casserole dish. Coat the meat in the flour and fry it in the hot oil until brown on all sides, then remove it and put it to one side while you gently fry the onions in the same fat, scraping the remnants of meat into the onions.

When the onions have softened slightly, add the carrot, stock, bay leaves and rosemary and put the meat back into the casserole dish, mixing it into the vegetables. Bring to the boil and cover the casserole dish, then place it in the preheated oven.

The mutton should take about 2½ hours to cook, but lamb will take less time.

While the meat is cooking, drain and rinse the peas, then bring to the boil in fresh water. Turn down the heat and simmer for about 45 minutes, or until soft. Drain and set aside. (If using canned peas, omit this entire stage.)

When the meat is very tender, skim any unwanted fat from the surface and then add the cooked peas to the stew. Reheat thoroughly, stir in the vinegar and mint, then season with salt and pepper and serve with buttered crusty bread.

Hoppin' John

Black-eyed beans/peas were brought to the American Deep South by African slaves in the 17th century. Much later, the term 'soul food' was coined to describe this Afro-American fusion and Hoppin' John, a classic combination of beans and rice cooked with onions, green (bell) pepper and celery, is possibly the most celebrated soul food dish of all. Hoppin' John is traditionally eaten at New Year in the Deep South to ensure good luck for the coming year. 'Eat poor on New Year's and eat fat for the rest of the year', the saying goes. It is often served with cornbread, so I have adapted that idea by putting sweetcorn kernels into the dish.

250 g/8 oz. dried black-eyed beans/peas, soaked overnight
1 ham hock (approximately 500 g/1 lb. in weight), preferably smoked, or 200 g/ 7 oz. smoked gammon, bacon or pancetta, in one piece
2 onions, chopped
1 green (bell) pepper, deseeded and diced
1 celery stick/rib, trimmed and diced
2 fresh or dried bay leaves
1 teaspoon dried thyme
½ teaspoon chilli/hot red pepper flakes
2 corn cobs or 200 g/1½ cups frozen sweetcorn/corn kernels, drained
250 g/1¼ cups long-grain rice
salt and cayenne pepper
2 tablespoons chopped spring onions/scallions or fresh chives or flat-leaf parsley, to garnish
Tabasco or other hot pepper sauce, to serve

Serves 4

Drain the black-eyed beans/peas and bring to the boil in a saucepan of fresh water, then simmer for 10 minutes and drain again.

Put the ham, gammon, bacon or pancetta in a large saucepan, cover with water and bring to the boil. Simmer for about 1 hour, then add the drained beans/peas, onions, green (bell) pepper, celery, bay leaves, thyme and chilli/hot red pepper flakes and bring back to the boil. Cover the pan and continue to cook very slowly for another 1½–2 hours, until the beans/peas are thoroughly cooked and the ham is falling off the bone.

Take the ham, gammon, bacon or pancetta out of the pan, and use a fork to shred the meat roughly, discarding any skin, bone and surplus fat. Return the meat to the pan.

With a sharp knife, scrape the kernels off the corn cobs into the pan or add the frozen sweetcorn/kernels. Simmer for another 15 minutes.

If there seems to be too much liquid, strain the stock into another saucepan and boil vigorously for a few minutes to reduce and concentrate the flavour. Return enough of the stock to the pan to moisten the vegetables, reserving the rest for soup another day.

Cook the rice in a separate saucepan according to the instructions on the packet.

Season the stew to taste with salt and cayenne pepper. Serve portions of rice in shallow soup bowls, topped with a mound of beans, ham, gammon, bacon or pancetta and vegetables in the centre of each. Sprinkle liberally with the spring onions/scallions, chopped chives or parsley, and serve with Tabasco or other hot sauce on the side.

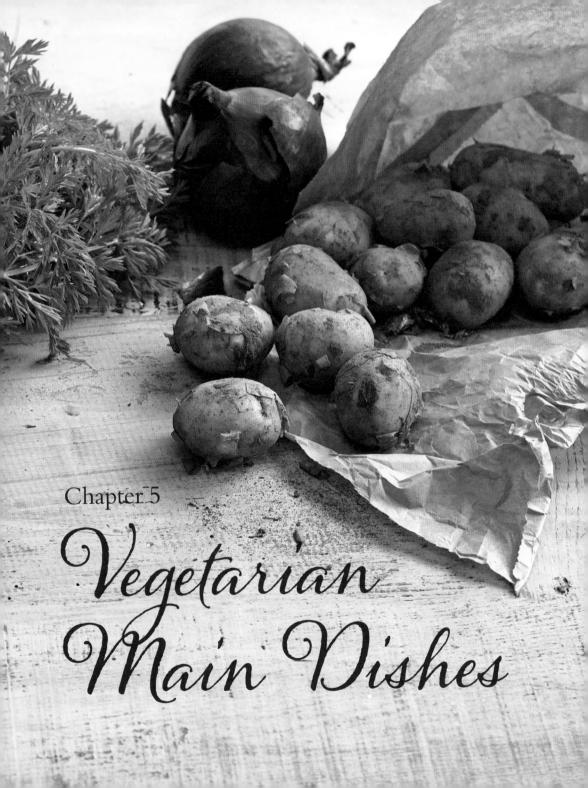

Chapter 5

Vegetarian Main Dishes

Mrs Harwood's cheese and lentil pie

Mrs Harwood's daughter donated this recipe to the cooks at the Imperial War Museum's café in London, where it became one of the most popular dishes on the menu. Dating from the Second World War, when rationing was in force and meat was scarce, it is more of a baked dish than a pie in the usual sense, and guaranteed to get a good reception as it comes out of the oven, crisp and golden on top.

300 g/1½ cups dried red lentils
30 g/2 tablespoons butter
1 onion, chopped
900 ml/3¾ cups milk
125 g/4 oz. Cheddar cheese, grated
2 tablespoons breadcrumbs
salt and ground black pepper

Serves 4

Rinse the lentils and soak in cold water for 1 hour, then drain.

Melt the butter in a medium-sized saucepan, and fry the onion very gently until soft and beginning to brown. This will take about 15 minutes.

Next, pour the milk into the pan and add the drained lentils, then stir around and bring to the boil. Once it has boiled, turn down the heat and simmer, uncovered, until the lentils are soft, which will take about an hour. Stir the mixture from time to time to prevent it sticking to the bottom of the pan, and if the liquid seems to be evaporating too fast, half-cover the pan, or top up with a little hot water, but don't let the mixture become too sloppy. It should be the texture of loose porridge/oatmeal when it is cooked.

Set the oven to 180°C (350°F) Gas 4.

When the lentils are cooked, season to taste with a little salt – don't overdo the salt as the cheese is salty – and pepper. Stir in half of the grated cheese.

Butter a gratin dish with a capacity of at least 1 litre/4 cups, and spoon the lentil and cheese mixture into the dish. Mix together the breadcrumbs and remaining cheese, then sprinkle over the top.

Bake in the oven for about 20–30 minutes, until the top is nicely crisp and golden. Serve immediately.

Roasted root vegetables would make a good accompaniment, the sweetness balancing the saltiness of the cheese.

Oven-baked Greek butter beans

The beans of choice for this dish are Greek *gigantes*, aptly named as they are huge butter beans that can be up to 4 cm/1½ in. long once they are soaked. Baked in the oven until meltingly soft in a rich, sweet tomato sauce, this is truly a Greek classic.

250 g/1½ cups dried *gigantes* beans, or butter/lima beans, soaked in water for 24 hours
1 fresh or dried bay leaf
1 large red onion, thinly sliced
3 garlic cloves, finely chopped
3 tablespoons olive oil, plus extra to serve
1 teaspoon dried oregano
½ teaspoon ground cinnamon
500 g/1 lb. vine-ripened tomatoes, skinned and chopped
2 teaspoons clear honey
2 tablespoons tomato purée/paste
2 tablespoons chopped fresh oregano, flat-leaf parsley, basil or dill
salt and ground black pepper
feta cheese, to serve
crusty bread, to serve

Serves 6

Drain the beans, and put in a saucepan with fresh water to cover. Bring to the boil and boil fairly vigorously for 10 minutes, then drain again. With fresh water and the bay leaf, bring back to the boil and simmer very gently for 45 minutes, until the beans are quite tender but not fully cooked. Take off the heat and leave in the liquid.

Preheat the oven to 160°C (325°F) Gas 3.

While the beans are cooking, gently sauté the onion and garlic in the olive oil in another saucepan, until they soften and smell sweet. Stir in the dried oregano, cinnamon, tomatoes, honey and tomato purée/paste and simmer together for 10 minutes.

Drain the beans, retaining the liquid.

Place the drained beans and tomato sauce in an ovenproof earthenware or cast-iron casserole dish, and stir well. Do not add salt at this stage. Heat the liquid in which the beans have cooked and pour enough of it over the contents of the casserole dish to barely cover the beans.

Bake the casserole, uncovered, in the oven for about 50 minutes, until the beans and the other vegetables are soft and thoroughly cooked, and the sauce is quite thick and concentrated. Check from time to time, and add a little more of the bean cooking liquid or a drizzle of olive oil if necessary to prevent everything drying out, but don't drown it. Season with salt and pepper, stir in the fresh herbs and serve with feta cheese, good crusty bread and additional olive oil to sprinkle over the beans.

Lentil moussaka

Popular throughout the Balkans, moussaka came to Britain in the fifties, and was received with such enthusiasm that it became almost a part of the national cuisine. This is a vegetarian version of a dish that normally includes minced/ground beef or lamb. It makes a good supper dish, served with nothing but a green salad and good bread.

500 g/1 lb. aubergines/eggplants
about 6 tablespoons olive oil
1 onion, finely chopped
1 leek, trimmed and chopped
3 garlic cloves, chopped
1 carrot, peeled and finely diced
6 tomatoes (about 750 g/1⅔ lbs.), peeled and chopped
4 tablespoons tomato purée/paste
½ teaspoon ground cinnamon
1 tablespoon dried oregano
2 fresh or dried bay leaves
1 teaspoon caster/granulated sugar
200 g/1 cup dried Puy/French green lentils
200 g/2 cups Pecorino cheese, grated
salt and ground black pepper

For the topping:

3 eggs, beaten
30 g/¼ cup plain/all-purpose flour
500 ml/16 fl. oz. Greek yogurt
1 teaspoon salt
ground black pepper
grated nutmeg

Serves 6

Preheat the oven to 180°C (350°F) Gas 4.

Cut the aubergines/eggplants into 1-cm/⅜-in. slices, and brush the cut sides with olive oil. Heat a baking sheet with sides in the oven for 5 minutes, then bake the aubergine/eggplant slices, sprinkled with a little salt, for about 30 minutes, until beginning to brown. Halfway through cooking, turn them over with a spatula, so they cook evenly.

Meanwhile, heat 3 tablespoons of the olive oil in a frying pan/skillet and fry the onion, leek and garlic over a gentle heat until soft and golden. Add the diced carrot, chopped tomatoes, tomato purée/paste, cinnamon, oregano and bay leaves, cover and simmer together for another 30 minutes or so. Stir in the sugar.

While the tomato sauce is cooking, rinse and drain the lentils, then place in a saucepan covered with cold water. Bring to the boil and simmer for about 20 minutes, until soft (bear in mind that they will not cook any further once mixed with the tomato sauce.) Drain the lentils and add to the tomato sauce, then season with salt and pepper.

Generously butter a deep ovenproof dish measuring 28 x 18 cm/ 11 x 7 in., and spread half of the aubergine/eggplant slices in the bottom. Cover with half of the tomato and lentil mixture, then repeat with another layer of each. Sprinkle half of the grated cheese over the surface.

To make the topping, whisk the eggs with the flour, then gently stir in the yogurt, salt and some pepper and the grated nutmeg.

Spoon the mixture over the dish of vegetables, finishing by sprinkling the remaining grated cheese over the surface.

Bake in the preheated oven for 30–40 minutes, until the top is bubbling and brown.

Persian pilgrim's soup

Soup in the Persian kitchen is a substantial affair, a meal in itself rather than a prelude of things to come. This restorative pottage, *ash-e-reshteh*, is one of the glories of Persian cuisine. It is traditionally served on the evening before the departure of pilgrims on their journey to Mecca, or in thanks for an act of God such as the recovery of a family member from illness. The noodles represent the tangled threads of life. Most of the ingredients can be varied according to taste and to what is available, but generous quantities of fresh herbs are essential – this is a dish that tastes as if it's doing you good. Make sure that some of the pulses are large ones that stay whole, and the rest – moong dal and lentils – are smaller, faster-cooking ones that disintegrate and thicken the soup.

2 tablespoons olive oil
1 onion, sliced
1 leek, trimmed and chopped
1 teaspoon ground turmeric
60 g/⅓ cup dried moong dal,
   rinsed and drained
or 60 g/⅓ cup dried red lentils,
   rinsed and drained
60 g/⅓ cup whole dried
   mung beans
200 g/7 oz. spinach leaves
a large bunch of fresh flat-leaf
   parsley and/or coriander/
   cilantro
dried dill and oregano (optional)
250 g/1¼ cups mixture of cooked
   butter/lima beans, chickpeas
   (garbanzos) and kidney beans
100 g/3½ oz. Iranian noodles
   (*reshteh* or *rishta*) or Italian
   linguine
salt and ground black pepper
sour cream, plain yogurt or *labne*
   (Middle Eastern strained
   yogurt), to serve
1 lemon or lime, cut into
   wedges, to serve
fried caramelized onions
   (optional), to serve

Heat the olive oil in a large pan and soften the onion gently, until golden brown. Stir in the chopped leek and cook for another few minutes, then add the turmeric and heat through to release its aroma. Add 1.5 litres/6 cups of water (or stock), then tip in the moong dal or lentils and the whole mung beans, bring back to the boil, covered, and simmer for about 1 hour, until the pulses are soft.

Meanwhile, pick over the spinach leaves and parsley and/or coriander, strip off the tough stalks and then wash the leaves. They can be dried in a salad spinner. Chop the leaves roughly.

When the moong dal/lentils are cooked, add the cooked beans and chickpeas to the pot and simmer for about another 20 minutes. Stir in the chopped herbs and spinach and more water if necessary, bring back to the boil, then drop in the noodles and simmer for another 15 minutes, or until the noodles are cooked.

Adjust the seasoning, then serve with sour cream, plain yogurt or *labne*, and quarters of lemon or lime to squeeze in as desired.

Fried caramelized onions are often spooned over at the end.

Split pea stew with Ethiopian spices

Sharing food is an important part of life in Ethiopia, where it is the custom for everyone to help themsleves to fragrant, spicy stews placed in mounds on a large pancake or *injera,* which acts both as a communal plate and an eating tool.

250 g/1¼ cups yellow split peas,
    rinsed thoroughly and drained
2 tablespoons olive oil
20 g/4 teaspoons butter
3 onions, finely chopped
3 garlic cloves, finely chopped
1 tablespoon of grated ginger
1 teaspoon cardamom seeds,
    crushed
1 teaspoon turmeric
250 g/8 oz. spinach, cooked,
    drained and chopped (optional)
a handful of torn fresh basil leaves
salt and ground black pepper

For the injera pancakes:
100 g/scant cup buckwheat or
    teff flour
1 egg, lightly beaten
300 ml/1¼ cups skimmed milk
30 g/2 tablespoons melted butter
a pinch of salt
sunflower oil, for frying

Serves 4-6

Simmer the split peas in a saucepan with 600 ml/2½ cups of fresh water for about 50 minutes, until they are tender and beginning to break up.

Meanwhile, in a frying pan/skillet, heat the oil and butter and fry the onion over a gentle heat until translucent and sweet smelling.

Add the garlic and ginger to the pan/skillet, then continue to cook for another 5 minutes, taking care that they don't burn. Stir in the cardamom and turmeric and cook for another 1–2 minutes.

Drain the cooked peas, retaining any cooking water that is left, and stir into the onions and spices. Season with salt and plenty of black pepper, then cover the pan and cook over a low heat for another 20–30 minutes, until the flavours have melded. Stir in the spinach (if using), heat through briefly, add the basil leaves, and serve. The stew should be solid enough to scoop up with the *injera,* but may need extra water adding as it cooks.

To make the *injera,* sift the flour and salt into a bowl and stir in the egg. Add the milk bit by bit, then beat the mixture until smooth. Set aside in a warm place for at least 1 hour. Stir the melted butter into the batter. Heat a pancake pan or frying pan/skillet and brush with a little oil, then pour a half-ladleful of batter onto the hot pan, rolling it around to spread the batter thinly over the surface. Cook over a medium heat until the bottom is brown then turn over and cook the other side. The batter will make 5–6 pancakes depending on the size of the pan.

Feasting and Fasting

On a journey around the Greek Islands in the 1960s, my friends and I got wind one day of a religious festival to be held at a remote church in the mountains some six hours' walk away, and we decided to go.

Scrambling along the narrow stony path through olive groves and herby scrub, we came across other pilgrims, but nothing prepared us for the huge crowd that had already gathered in the whitewashed square in front of the church by the time we arrived in late afternoon.

As dusk fell, a fire was lit beneath several huge cauldrons, and villagers filled the pots with beans, tomatoes, onions and wild herbs, with the odd chunk of boney meat for flavour, then stirred it all around with wooden spoons the size of spades and left the fragrant mixture to simmer for several hours. The scent of the wood fire mingling with the cooking and incense drifting from the tiny church was intoxicating.

At last it was ready and once the liturgical celebrations were over, bowls appeared from nowhere, vast loaves of fresh crusty bread were cut into chunks and everybody was fed, including us intruders on this scene. Festivals of this kind have taken place since the beginning of time, nicely combining the secular pleasures of a good party with the observance of religious belief. From that day on, I have never failed to appreciate the value of beans as a source of sustenance and comfort. Because of their ability to feed crowds at little cost, pulses feature widely in communal feasts. In Sicily, it is still the custom to eat *macco di San Giuseppe*, a soup made of dried broad/fava beans and other legumes, on St Joseph's Day, 19th March, in remembrance of when the saint intervened to end a drought which had threatened to cause a catastrophic famine. The feast conveniently falls just at the time when winter stores of dried pulses would need to be finished off in preparation for the new season's crop, and a simple meal is often

prepared from these leftovers and served to all and sundry at a ritual banquet.

Though a pagan festival, New Year's Eve is another time for feasting, and eating legumes is often an essential part of the celebration. Linked with the symbolism of fertility, the embryo and growth, they are associated with the bringing of good luck.

No Italian New Year's Eve celebration is complete without *cotechino con lenticchie* – a delicious pork sausage served on a bed of lentils, which symbolize coins and by implication money and so are thought to guarantee a prosperous year ahead. The more lentils you eat, it is thought, the richer you will become. In the American Deep South, it is Hoppin' John, a hearty stew of black-eyed beans, ham hock and green (bell) pepper which brings luck, traditionally eaten on New Year's Day.

In Japanese folklore, beans of all kinds are considered good luck. Stewed black beans are served as part of the New Year's feast as a symbol of fertility, while rice with purple adzuki beans is a festive dish at many events throughout the year.

As well as feasting, pulses are also associated with ritual fasting, or rather abstinence from meat, which is often misleadingly referred to as fasting. In communities where abstinence is practised on a regular basis, people invariably enjoy a greater variety of vegetarian dishes, often based on pulses as they become the main source of protein in the diet.

The extraordinary range and sophistication of Indian vegetarian cookery and the importance of pulses in the subcontinent arose not just from poverty but from the vegetarian requirements of the Hindu religion. In Ethiopia, abstinence from meat is stipulated amongst the Coptic Christian community on the huge number of fasting days when pulses form the centrepiece of most meals. Similarly, in Mediterranean countries, where from the early days of Christianity, fasting and abstinence have also been practised – during Lent, on Wednesdays and Fridays and on other occasions through the year – there is an abundance of dishes based on beans, chickpeas and lentils.

The Protestants of Northern Europe and North America tended to favour dried peas during Lent, often in the form of soup. In Lancashire and Yorkshire on Carling or Care Sunday, the fourth or fifth Sunday in Lent, people traditionally ate black Carling (maple) peas. There is a saying in Yorkshire, which promises that those who eat pancakes on Shrove Tuesday and dried peas on Ash Wednesday will have money in their pockets all the year.

Food plays an important part in the Jewish calendar of Sabbath and festivals, and pulses feature in a number of dishes which have ritual significance. Beans are an essential ingredient of the Ashkenazi Jewish Sabbath dish *cholent*, a slow-cooked stew of meat, potatoes, barley and beans, somewhat similar to cassoulet. It could be prepared the day before, simmered slowly overnight and reheated the following day, in accordance with Jewish law which forbids work on the Sabbath.

The Sephardi Jewish version of *cholent*, known as *dafina* or *adafina*, is very similar but tends to have Mediterranean ingredients. In Morocco it is known as *skhena*, where it is made with chickpeas and flavoured with cinnamon and nutmeg.

In 1492, the same year that Christopher Columbus discovered the New World, King Ferdinand of Spain issued an edict expelling all Jews from Spain, resulting in large-scale loss of life and property. Many Jews converted to Christianity so that they could remain in Spain, but they continued to prepare *adafina*, substituting pork for kosher meats, and the new beans brought back by Columbus from the Americas for chickpeas in regions where chickpeas were not available. The most famous Spanish bean dish of all, *cocido*, is said to have evolved from *adafina*, and is served to this day every Wednesday in Madrid restaurants.

Jews also cook black-eyed beans at their New Year festivities as a symbol of plenty and fertility, while the Moroccan Jewish community serves *bessara*, a broad/fava bean soup, at Passover, as a commemoration of the meal that the Hebrews ate in Egypt.

Mention should also be made of the Jewish custom of serving lentils at the meal of condolence, which is prepared for the mourners after a death has taken place, but before the funeral. Lentils, being round, symbolize the cycle of life that never stops, of which suffering and dying form a part. Similarly, in Parsi communities of western India, dhansak, a dish of lamb and lentils, is served on days when ancestors and departed souls are remembered.

On a more cheerful note, Hippocrates, the father of medicine, is said to have recommended lentils to keep a man virile well into old age and Plutarch thought that regular consumption of fassolatha, Greek bean soup, was the way to a strong libido.

Beans were a symbol of regeneration. They could even lead from abject poverty to untold wealth if, like Jack, you had the good fortune to come by a magic bean, with the power to transport you to heaven where you could marry a princess and live happily ever after.

Stew of borlotti beans with fennel

The use of fennel reminds me of Sicily, where the wild herb grows
everywhere, and the leaves are used to flavour *pasta con le sarde* (pasta with
sardines) as well as sausages and cured meats. Fennel calms flatulence – fennel
oil is used in the manufacture of babies' gripe water – so its digestive properties
make it the ideal companion for beans. This comforting stew works perfectly as
a vegetarian dish, but could equally well be cooked with the addition of some
cubed pork shoulder or bacon, rubbed with crushed fennel seeds, which
should be browned in the pan with the onion and fennel wedges.

1 large or 2 small fennel bulbs
1 tablespoon olive oil
150 g/5 oz. small onion or large
  shallot, chopped
2 garlic cloves, crushed
1 x 400-g/14-oz. can chopped
  tomatoes
100 ml/⅓ cup red wine
250 g/1¼ cups cooked, soaked
  dried borlotti beans, or the
  contents of 1 x 400-g/14-oz.
  can, drained
1 teaspoon fennel seeds, crushed
2–3 fresh sage leaves
1 fresh or dried bay leaf
bread rolls, to serve

Serves 2

Trim the fennel, making sure to keep any green feathery fronds for
strewing later. Cut it into wedges, leaving the base intact so that it
holds the leaves together while they cook.

Heat the oil in a medium-sized frying pan/skillet, and gently brown
the onion or shallot and fennel, then add crushed garlic cloves and
cook for another 1–2 minutes.

Add the tomatoes, wine, beans, fennel seeds, sage and bay leaf. Cover
the pan/skillet and cook gently for about 40 minutes.

Sprinkle with the chopped fennel fronds and serve with bread rolls.

Red beans à la bourguignonne

Thumbing through a 1963 edition of *Larousse Gastronomique*, I came across a sketchy recipe for red beans in red wine *à la bourguignonne*, and what follows is based on that idea, a variation of the classic beef stew that was once staple *bistrot* fare. By omitting the bacon, the dish makes a splendid vegetarian main course. It's great with chunks of crusty bread, to mop up the juices.

175 g/1 cup dried red beans, soaked overnight and drained, or the contents of 1½ x 400-g/ 14-oz. cans, drained

100 g/3½ oz. smoked bacon lardons (optional)

15 g/1 tablespoon olive oil or butter

10 baby onions or shallots, peeled, but left whole

2 carrots, peeled and diced

2 garlic cloves, 1 crushed and 1 finely chopped

250 g/8 oz. button mushrooms

150 ml/⅔ cup red wine

150 ml/⅔ cup well-flavoured vegetable stock

1 fresh or dried bay leaf

a small bunch of fresh flat-leaf parsley, finely chopped

½ celery stick/rib, trimmed

a sprig of fresh thyme, or 1 teaspoon dried thyme

15 g/1 tablespoon butter

salt and ground black pepper

sugar, to taste (optional)

Serves 4

Cook the soaked beans in a saucepan of boiling water for 10 minutes, drain and replace with fresh water. Bring back to the boil, and simmer very gently for 30 minutes. Omit this entire stage if using canned beans.

Meanwhile, sauté the lardons of smoked bacon in a frying pan/skillet with the oil or butter until brown or omit for the vegetarian option.

Remove the bacon with a slotted spatula and set aside. Over a gentle heat, fry the baby onions or shallots and the carrots in the same pan until they begin to brown. Stir in the crushed garlic and continue to cook for 1–2 minutes, until the garlic no longer smells raw.

Add the mushrooms and fry them until tender and lightly browned, then pour in the red wine, bring to the boil and simmer for 5 minutes.

Put the bacon back into the pan and add the stock and the beans with enough of their cooking water to cover. Add the bay leaf, the parsley stalks, celery and thyme, pushed down well so that they are covered with liquid. Cover tightly and simmer gently for 2–3 hours (or 1 hour if using canned beans), until the beans are thoroughly cooked and and the flavours are blended. This can be done on the hob/stovetop, or in an oven at 150°C (300°F) Gas 2 in an ovenproof casserole dish with a tight-fitting lid.

Check the seasoning and add salt and pepper to taste, plus a pinch or two of sugar if necessary to counteract the acidity of the wine.

Blend the butter with the parsley leaves and the chopped garlic, and stir into the casserole dish just before serving.

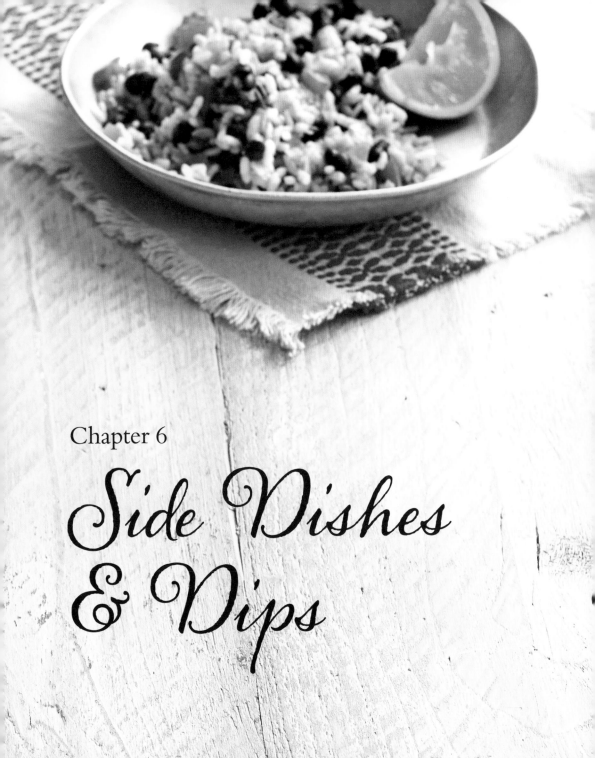

Chapter 6

Side Dishes & Dips

Black-eyed beans and squash in coconut milk

A mildly spiced vegetarian recipe from Kerala, *olan* is served as a side dish with other vegetable or meat curries.

250 g /1¼ cups ash gourd (winter melon) or butternut squash, peeled, deseeded and cubed
1–4 green chillies/chiles, deseeded and finely chopped
1 teaspoon cumin seeds, lightly crushed
250 g/8 oz. cooked, soaked dried black-eyed beans/peas or the contents of 1 x 400-g/14-oz. can, drained
150 ml/⅔ cup coconut milk
2 teaspoons coconut oil or sunflower oil
1 teaspoon mustard seeds
a few curry leaves, fresh if possible, otherwise use dried
4 shallots, thinly sliced
salt

Serves 4–5

In a saucepan, simmer the squash, chillies/chiles and cumin in 200 ml/¾ cup water for about 10 minutes until the squash is soft. Season with salt.

Add the black-eyed beans/peas and coconut milk, and a little water if necessary to cover the vegetables, then cover and simmer for another 10 minutes.

In a frying pan/skillet, heat the oil and fry the mustard seeds, curry leaves and sliced shallots until the shallots are beginning to brown.

Stir these into the black-eyed beans/peas and squash, add more salt to taste and serve.

Moong dal with coconut parippu

A soothing South Indian dish, which can either be a soup or a stew to serve with rice, according to how much water is used.

175 g/a scant cup dried moong dal, rinsed
½ teaspoon ground turmeric
50 g/¾ cup grated fresh coconut, or 25 g/⅓ cup dessicated coconut soaked in a little warm water for 5 minutes
2 shallots, chopped
3 green chillies/chiles, sliced
½ teaspoon cumin seeds
salt

For the seasoning

2 tablespoons vegetable oil
1 teaspoon black mustard seeds
2 shallots, sliced
2 whole dried red chillies/chiles
10 fresh curry leaves

Serves 4

Rinse and drain the moong dal, then put in a saucepan with the turmeric and 750 ml/3 cups of water. Bring to the boil, then simmer, covered, for about 20 minutes or until the dal is very tender.

While the dal is cooking, use a blender to grind together the coconut, shallots, green chillies/chiles and cumin seeds, adding a little water if necessary to make a thick and smooth paste. When the dal has been simmering for 20 minutes, stir this paste into it and continue to cook for another 10 minutes. Add salt to taste and continue to cook gently while you fry the seasoning.

In another frying pan/skillet, heat the oil, and when it is medium hot, add the mustard seeds. When they start to pop, add the shallots and fry until brown. Next add the chillies/chiles and then the curry leaves, before tipping the whole lot into the dal.

Serve as a stew with rice, or dilute with water and serve as a soup with naan bread.

Succotash (Bean, corn and squash stew)

The name succotash comes from *m'sick-quotash*, the Native American word for a mixture of sweetcorn and butter/lima beans, which was adapted by colonists to include other vegetables, as well as salt pork or boiling fowl. This is a vegetarian version with squash and sage. Succotash does not usually contain squash, but beans, corn and squash are traditionally grown together, a system known known as the 'Three Sisters'. A perfect example of companion planting, the maize/corn stalks form the support for climbing beans, while the squash trail on the ground below, their large leaves suppressing weeds and conserving moisture at the same time. Because the plants support and protect each other, Native Americans believe that by eating the three vegetables together, they will in turn be protected.

1 small butternut squash, peeled, deseeded and cut into bite-sized chunks
3 tablespoons sunflower oil
10 fresh sage leaves, 5 left whole and 5 shredded
30 g/2 tablespoons butter
1 onion, chopped
kernels from 2 corn cobs, scraped off with a sharp knife, or 250 g/1½ cups drained, canned or frozen sweetcorn
2 teaspoons dried oregano
1 red chilli/chile, deseeded and chopped (optional)
250 g/1¼ cups cooked, soaked dried butter/lima beans, or the contents of 1 x 400-g/14-oz. can, drained
3 tomatoes, halved horizontally
3 tablespoons double/heavy cream
salt and ground black pepper
chopped/snipped fresh chives or flat-leaf parsley, to garnish

In a large bowl, toss the squash cubes in 2 tablespoons of the oil, season with salt and pepper and add the whole sage leaves. Transfer to a baking sheet and roast in the oven at 200°C (400° F) Gas 6 for 45–60 minutes, until the squash cubes are soft and the edges are beginning to brown. Set aside.

Meanwhile, in a large frying pan/skillet, heat the remaining oil with the butter and fry the onion over a gentle heat until soft. Stir in the corn, the rest of the sage, the oregano and chilli/chile, then add the beans and a little water. Heat gently and simmer, covered, for 5 minutes. Add the roast squash (discard the sage, which will be charred), grate the flesh of the tomatoes into the stew (discard the skin) and check the seasoning.

Cover the pan and heat everything through, then stir in the cream. Strew with chopped chives or parsley and serve.

Serves 4

Moors and Christians

Also known as *congri*, this predominantly Cuban dish is found in various guises all over Central America and the Caribbean, and also in southern Spain. The Spanish name, *Moros y Cristianos* (Moors and Christians), refers to the Muslim conquest of the Iberian peninsula, and may also allude to some kind of eventual integration of the two cultures in the mixture of black beans and white rice.

At its most basic, the dish consists simply of black beans and rice, but many more elaborate versions exist with a variety of additional ingredients. Although it is traditional to mix the bean cooking liquid into the rice, resulting in a speckled appearance, I prefer the stark visual contrast of black beans and white rice. The addition of allspice and sour orange add a piquancy to the dish but are not traditional, although both are widely grown in the Caribbean. Allspice is so called because it seems to combine the flavours of cinnamon, cloves and nutmeg, and is native to tropical America. It should be used judiciously or the flavour of cloves will overwhelm all others, but in this dish it adds a wonderfully aromatic touch.

3 tablespoons olive oil
½ onion, finely chopped
4 garlic cloves, finely chopped
1 green (bell) pepper, deseeded and finely chopped
1 teaspoon cumin seeds, roasted and crushed
¾ teaspoon ground allspice
200 g/1 cup short-grain rice, such as Bomba, rinsed and drained
125 g/⅔ cup dried black beans, soaked overnight and boiled for 45 minutes–1 hour with ½ chopped onion, 2 garlic cloves and 1 fresh bay leaf, or the contents of 1 x 400-g/ 14-oz. can, drained
grated zest and freshly squeezed juice of ½ lime or Seville orange
salt and ground black pepper

Serves 4

Heat the oil in a saucepan, and sauté the onion gently for about 10 minutes, then add the garlic, green (bell) pepper, cumin and allspice. Cook very gently for another 10–15 minutes, until the onion is golden and the (bell) pepper is soft.

Meanwhile, cook the rice according to the packet instructions, then drain and keep warm.

When the beans are cooked, strain and add to the onion and pepper sofrito. Stir in the zest and juice of the lime or orange, season with salt and pepper, reheat gently and then very carefully combine the beans with the cooked rice.

Refried beans

The English name of this Mexican staple is a bit of a misnomer, arising from the fact that 'refried beans' is a historic mistranslation of the Spanish *frijoles refritos*. The beans are not actually refried, but boiled and then fried. At its most basic and traditional, the dish is made by simply mashing cooked beans into a frying pan/skillet of hot lard, a spoonful at a time, adding a little cooking liquid as you go, then simmering until the right consistency is reached – similar to mashed potatoes. Here, I have substituted sunflower or olive oil for the lard, and given added flavour by frying onions and other ingredients in the oil, before adding the beans. Either way, the dish is so delicious that it's easy to understand how a whole nation became addicted to it. Any leftovers will keep well in the fridge for several days, and can be reheated gently with a little more oil.

250 g/1½ cups dried pinto beans, soaked overnight, or the contents of 1 x 400-g/14-oz. can, drained
1 fresh or dried bay leaf
6–8 tablespoons sunflower or olive oil, or 85–115 g/⅓–½ cup lard
1 onion, peeled and chopped
3 garlic cloves, chopped
2 fresh green chillies/chiles, deseeded and chopped
1 teaspoon dried oregano or Mexican epazote
½ teaspoon ground cumin
salt and ground black pepper
crumbled Lancashire cheese, soft curd cheese or sour cream, tortillas and salsa, or tortilla chips, to serve

Serves 4

In a large saucepan, boil the soaked dried beans and the bay leaf in a minimal amount of fresh water, just to cover, for about 1 hour or until tender. Drain them, reserving the liquid. If using canned beans, drain and use water or stock in place of the bean cooking liquid.

Heat the oil or lard in a frying pan/skillet and add the onion, garlic and the chillies/chiles. Sauté gently for about 10 minutes.

Take a ladleful of the cooked beans and mash them into the other ingredients in the frying pan/skillet. Stir in the oregano or epazote and cumin and cook for another 1–2 minutes.

Tip the contents of the frying pan/skillet into the remaining beans, season with salt and pepper and stir in a little of the cooking liquid. Simmer over a low heat for another 30 minutes or so – exact timing is not important here – until the sauce has thickened and the mixture has the consistency of mashed potato. You may need to add more liquid as it cooks.

Season to taste and serve rolled in tortillas with crumbled Lancashire cheese, soft curd cheese or sour cream and salsa, as a side dish, or as a dip with tortilla chips.

Purée of fava beans and sautéed chicory

This soft, creamy mixture of puréed fava beans and boiled greens had its origins in ancient Egypt, and today is found in Puglia, southern Italy, where it is called *'ncapriata* or *fave e cicoria*. A similar dish, *macco*, is served in Sicily, and it is often mixed with wild fennel. The dish is a direct descendant of the thick pottage of legumes that has nourished peasants and farmers for many thousands of years, yet to this day appears on the menu of almost every fashionable restaurant in Puglia. The purée itself is made from split dried fava beans – *fave sgusciate* – which are already shelled (in the UK and the US, they can be bought in Middle Eastern grocery stores and delicatessens.) They have the advantage of needing no preliminary soaking, and break up in cooking to the point where they can be beaten to a purée with a wooden spoon, although a blender makes shorter work of the same process. In Italy, the boiled greens are usually wild chicory, but Swiss chard or young dandelion leaves would make good substitutes. All manner of variations exist, even for such a simple dish. The beans can be boiled alone, or with a potato, or can have mint or sautéed spring onions/scallions added, but the essential element is always the olive oil – the best you can find – which is beaten in at the end.

250 g/1¼ cups split dried fava beans
1 medium potato, peeled and diced
100 ml/½ cup olive oil, plus extra for sautéeing and to serve
500 g/1 lb. Swiss chard leaves
2 garlic cloves, crushed
salt
sourdough bread, to serve

Serves 4-6

In a large saucepan, boil the beans and potato in enough water to cover the beans by a few centimetres/a couple of inches, for about 1 hour. Add more boiling water during cooking if the mixture gets too dry. By the time the beans are cooked, most of the water should have been absorbed.

Beat in the olive oil until you have a thick, smooth purée, then season with salt.

Meanwhile, boil or steam the greens. While they are cooking, heat a tablespoon of olive oil in a frying pan/skillet, and gently sauté the garlic, taking care not to let it brown, then toss the drained greens in the garlicky oil. Serve alongside a good dollop of the purée, with extra olive oil on the side, and hunks of sourdough bread.

The simplest dal

In India, the word *dal* is used loosely to describe any type of split, hulled legume, but it has also come to refer to the comforting, creamy mush that is an essential part of any Indian meal. There are two distinct processes in preparing dal and both have infinite variations. First, the dal must be thoroughly rinsed, then boiled in water, to which flavourings such as turmeric, chilli, garlic and ginger may be added. Turmeric is almost indispensable, as it adds not only a vivid yellow colour and distinctive flavour but is thought to be a digestive aid. The final addition of the *tarka* – fried onion, garlic, chilli/chile or other ingredients, which are stirred, still sizzling, into the dal just before serving – can transform a rather bland boiled pulse into something delicious. Defying convention, this recipe was devised for busy people who like eating dal but are put off by the prospect of frying the tarka. It is full of flavour, fat-free and simplicity itself to prepare.

180 g/1 cup dried red lentils, thoroughly rinsed until the water is completely clear and drained
½ onion, finely chopped
2 garlic cloves, finely chopped
½ teaspoon finely chopped fresh ginger
1 teaspoon ground turmeric
¼ teaspoon chilli powder
1 teaspoon salt
2 green chillies/chiles, chopped*
freshly squeezed juice of ½ lime
large bunch of fresh coriander/ cilantro, chopped
boiled rice, to serve

Serves 4-6

Put the rinsed lentils in a saucepan with 450 ml/scant 2 cups of water and bring to the boil. Cover and simmer very gently for about 20 minutes, until the lentils are soft and mushy.

Add another 200 ml/a generous ¾ cup of water together with the onion, garlic, ginger, turmeric, chilli powder and salt. Bring back to the boil and simmer, covered, very gently for another 30 minutes.

Stir in the chopped fresh chilli/chile and simmer for another 10 minutes, then add the lime juice and coriander/cilantro. Allow to simmer for another 5 minutes, then serve with boiled rice.

* It is difficult to specify the amount and type of chilli/chile to add, as it depends on personal preference – chillies/chiles can be very sweet and mild or wildly hot, so choose them with care. If you want the flavour without the heat, then remove and discard the seeds.

Tarka

If you do want to add a tarka, heat 3 tablespoons of vegetable oil in a pan, add 1 dried red chilli/chile and 1 teaspoon of cumin seeds to the hot oil. Stir in ½ thinly sliced onion, and when nearly brown, add 1 thinly sliced garlic clove. When the garlic is beginning to brown, tip the whole lot into the cooked dal. If adding a tarka, reduce the amount of onion in the dal itself to ¼ onion and the garlic to 1 clove.

Lebanese houmus

There must be thousands of recipes for houmus, but this is the way Mohammed Alden, owner and chef of Al Waha, the popular Lebanese restaurant in Notting Hill, London, makes it. It isn't the quickest way to make houmus, but it may well be the best. He says houmus must have a smooth, velvety texture – this is essential – and the secret is threefold: skin the chickpeas, chill the ingredients before blending and add olive oil only just before serving. And no garlic.

200 g/1¼ cups dried chickpeas (garbanzos), soaked overnight and drained
½ teaspoon bicarbonate of/baking soda
60 ml/¼ cup very cold freshly squeezed lemon juice
60 g/¼ cup tahini (about 3 tablespoons)
salt
olive oil, paprika and chopped fresh flat-leaf parsley, to serve
hot pitta bread, to serve

Serves 4-6

Put the chickpeas in a large saucepan with double the amount of fresh water. Add the bicarbonate of/baking soda and bring to the boil, then simmer, covered, until the chickpeas are cooked – about 60–90 minutes.

Take the saucepan off the heat and put it under the cold water tap/faucet. This will shock the skins into cracking, so that they come off easily and float to the surface. Gently stir the chickpeas, and as the skins surface, remove them with a slotted spoon. Continue until most of the skins have been removed.

Strain the water from the chickpeas and leave in a colander in the fridge, preferably overnight, to drain thoroughly. Squeeze the lemon juice and chill in the fridge overnight, or add ice cubes for a quick chill.

Put the chickpeas into a food processor and blitz until you have a smooth paste, then add the tahini and process again. The mixture should be very smooth but still a little firm. Add the lemon juice and blend again, then add salt to taste.

Finally, leave the mixture for 15–20 minutes to allow the flavour to develop. If it is too thick, dilute with more lemon juice and ice.

Put the mixture in a dish, then make swirly grooves in the surface with the back of a spoon and drizzle with some olive oil. Sprinkle with paprika and chopped parsley, and serve with hot pitta bread.

It will keep perfectly well in the fridge, covered with clingfilm/plastic wrap, for several days.

Greek fava dip

One of the most popular appetizers in Greek tavernas is *fava*, a tasty dip made from tiny yellow split peas, called, rather confusingly, *fava*. These peas, *Lathyrus climenum*, have grown on the volcanic island of Santorini for the past 3,500 years. The plants, which resemble English sweet peas grown in gardens for their scented flowers, can also be found growing wild in other parts of the Mediterranean. Authentic Santorini *fava* comes with an IGP certification of origin, but demand outstrips the meagre supply, so it is hard, though not impossible, to find. Split yellow peas, however, make a good substitute.

50 ml/3 tablespoons olive oil
1 onion, finely diced
250 g/8 oz. dried Greek fava peas
   or dried yellow split peas
2 fresh or dried bay leaves
1 teaspoon dried oregano
salt and ground black pepper
freshly squeezed lemon juice,
   to taste
1 tablespoon pickled caper
   berries, drained, to serve
1 sweet red onion, very thinly
   sliced, or grilled artichoke
   hearts, cut in half, to serve
toasted pitta bread or
   breadsticks, to serve

Serves 6

Heat half of the olive oil in a saucepan and soften the diced onion. Add 500 ml/2 cups of water, bring to the boil and stir in the split peas. Add the bay leaves and the oregano and simmer, covered, for 1–2 hours, or until the water has been absorbed and the *fava* has become completely mushy. Stir from time to time to prevent it sticking to the bottom of the pan, and add more hot water if necessary.

When it is cooked, allow to cool slightly, remove the bay leaves, then blitz to a purée in a food processor. Stir in the rest of the olive oil, then season with salt, pepper and lemon juice to taste. Dilute with a little cold water to get the right consistency.

Serve cold in a shallow bowl, with the caper berries and onion slices or artichokes and toasted pitta bread or breadsticks to dip into the communal bowl.

Syrian aubergine and chickpea ragout
(Munazalit bathinjan)

A winning combination of roasted chunks of aubergine/eggplant and nutty chickpeas, bound together in a sweet tomato and onion sauce enriched with herbs and spices, this is one of those Mediterranean dishes that is at its best when served warm or at room temperature. It is popular in both Syria and Lebanon, where it is served with warm bread as part of a selection of mezze, or with rice or as an accompaniment to roasted or grilled meat.

2 medium aubergines/eggplants (about 500 g/1 lb. in total)
4 tablespoons olive oil
1 large onion, finely sliced
4 garlic cloves, finely sliced
½ teaspoon ground cinnamon
¼ teaspoon freshly grated nutmeg
a generous bunch of fresh flat-leaf parsley, chopped
4 tomatoes, skinned and chopped
250 g/1¼ cups cooked, soaked dried chickpeas (garbanzos), or the contents of 1 x 400-g/14-oz. can, drained
2 tablespoons chopped fresh mint
salt and ground black pepper
a generous bunch of fresh coriander/cilantro, chopped, to garnish
warm bread, to serve
plain yogurt, to serve

Serves 6

Preheat the oven to 180°C (350°F) Gas 4.

Cut the aubergines/eggplants into 2-cm/¾-in. cubes, and toss in half of the olive oil, then spread out on a baking sheet and roast in the oven for about 20 minutes, turning the pieces over once halfway through cooking, until fairly soft. Set aside.

Meanwhile, in a saucepan over a gentle heat, soften the sliced onion and garlic in the remaining olive oil, adding a couple of tablespoons of water if necessary to prevent browning. This should take about 20 minutes, until the onion is golden and melting.

Add the spices and stir around for 1–2 minutes to blend the flavours, then tip in the parsley, chopped tomatoes and aubergine/eggplant, followed by the drained chickpeas. Add about 200 ml/a generous ¾ cup water, bring to the boil and then simmer, covered, for 20–30 minutes.

Take off the heat, stir in the fresh mint, adjust the seasoning and set aside for 1–2 hours before serving. In fact, the dish keeps perfectly well for a good 24 hours, and may even improve, and can be easily reheated.

Season with salt and pepper, sprinkle with the chopped coriander/cilantro and serve warm with plain yogurt on the side.

Chapter 7

Desserts

Sweet Sicilian pastries

These lovely little pastries, called *cassateddi*, are a Sicilian speciality, typically enjoyed at Easter time. In other parts of the island they are filled with ricotta, but this version from the Palermo region has a stuffing of sweetened chickpea purée flavoured with cinnamon and punctuated with chocolate, nuts and candied citron peel. The candied peel is a substitute for *zuccata*, a Sicilian preserve made with summer squash. The addition of chopped almonds is more typical of the region around Enna, but they add a pleasing crunch to the texture. Traditionally, the flaky pastry is made with wine and lard, which is rolled very thinly and deep-fried, but this cheat's version uses ready-made sweet shortcrust pastry that is baked in the oven.

1 packet sweet shortcrust or puff pastry/pie dough (350 g/12½ oz.)

For the filling

250 g/1¼ cups cooked, soaked dried chickpeas (garbanzos), or the contents of 1 x 400-g/14-oz. can, drained and puréed
2 tablespoons clear honey
60 g/5 tablespoons caster/granulated sugar
50 g/⅓ cup almonds, toasted and chopped
1 teaspoon ground cinnamon
60 g/2 oz. dark/bittersweet chocolate, chopped
60 g/2 oz. diced candied citron peel
icing/confectioners' sugar, for sprinkling

Makes about 30

In a bowl, mix all of the ingredients for the filling well with a wooden spoon.

Preheat the oven to 180°C (350°F) Gas 4.

On a floured board, roll out the pastry, and cut out discs about 8 cm/3 in. in diameter. Place a teaspoonful of the filling in the centre of each disc, fold over and seal with your finger, to form half-moon shapes. Place on a greased baking sheet.

Repeat until all of the filling is used up, then bake the parcels in the preheated oven for about 20 minutes, until lightly browned.

Sprinkle with icing/confectioners' sugar, and serve warm.

Sweet fava bean tart

This delicious recipe is adapted from one given in *A Proper Newe Booke of Cookery*, dating from 1545.

100 g/⅔ cup shelled split dried fava beans
3 eggs, separated
250 g/8 oz. cottage or soft curd cheese
125 g/⅔ cup caster/granulated sugar
60 g/4 tablespoons butter, softened
30 g/¼ cup self-raising/rising flour
1 teaspoon ground cinnamon
2 tablespoons orange flower water
4 apricots, cut into quarters (optional)
icing/confectioners' sugar, for sprinkling

For the saffron pastry

a good pinch of saffron strands
125 g/1 cup plain/all-purpose flour
75 g/5 tablespoons butter, chilled and diced
75 g/2½ tablespoons caster/granulated sugar
1 egg yolk

Serves 8

Rinse the beans and boil for 10 minutes in a saucepan, then drain and put them back in the pan. Add 200 ml/a generous ¾ cup of fresh water and bring back to the boil, then simmer for another 30–40 minutes, until the beans have broken down almost into a purée. Leave to cool in the pan – as it cools, the purée will solidify.

To make the saffron pastry, first soak the saffron in 1 tablespoon of hot water and leave to cool. Put the flour and butter in a food processor and pulse briefly, until the mixture resembles breadcrumbs. Add the sugar and egg yolk, together with the saffron and its water, and blend until the mixture forms a ball. Wrap the pastry in clingfilm/plastic wrap and chill for at least 1 hour before using.

Preheat the oven to 180°C (350°F) Gas 4. When ready to bake the tart, on a floured board, roll out the pastry and use it to line a greased 23-cm/9-in. tart pan.

To make the bean filling, put the cooled bean purée, egg yolks, cottage or curd cheese, sugar, butter, flour, cinnamon and orange flower water in the food processor and beat until smooth. Transfer to a bowl.

Whisk the egg whites and carefully fold them into the bean mixture. Spoon the mixture into the pastry shell, arrange the apricot quarters over the surface, if using, and place the tart in the preheated oven. Bake for 35–40 minutes, until the filling is just set. Serve warm or at room temperature and sprinkle with icing/confectioners' sugar.

Noah's pudding

Legend has it that after the flood had subsided and Noah's Ark had come to rest on Mount Ararat, the survivors wished to hold a celebration as an expression of gratitude to God. Not surprisingly, the cupboards were somewhat bare, but this delicious Turkish dessert, made from the remains of the stores, was concocted for the occasion. Turkish food stores sell special wheat for making *asure*, as this dish is known, but quick-cook farro or spelt works perfectly too.

60 g/½ cup dried apricots, chopped
60 g/½ cup dark raisins
60 g/½ cup sultanas/golden raisins
75 g/⅔ cup quick-cook farro wheat
60 g/⅓ cup short-grain rice, such as pudding rice
125 g/⅔ cup cooked, soaked dried chickpeas (garbanzos), drained
125 g/⅔ cup cooked, soaked dried white beans, such as cannellini, drained
1 orange
75 g/⅓ cup caster/granulated sugar
1–2 tablespoons rose or orange flower water
1 pomegranate
75 g/½ cup pistachios, walnuts or almonds, chopped

Serves 6–8

Pour 200 ml/¾ cup of boiling water over the dried fruit and leave to soak for about 2 hours. At the same time, cover the wheat with cold water and leave to soak.

Drain the fruit, retaining the soaking liquid, and set aside.

Drain the wheat and put it in a saucepan with the rice, the liquid in which the dried fruit was soaked, and another 400 ml/1⅔ cups of water. Cover the pan and bring to the boil, then turn down the heat and simmer for 20 minutes, until the rice and wheat are soft.

Add the cooked chickpeas and beans to the pan, together with the soaked fruit. Cover the pan and bring to the boil, then simmer gently for another 15 minutes, stirring from time to time to prevent the mixture sticking to the pan, until it becomes like a thick porridge/oatmeal. Add extra boiling water if necessary.

While the mixture is cooking, peel the orange and, using a sharp knife, cut the segments away from the membrane. Cut each segment into thirds. Using a potato peeler, pare off thin pieces of orange zest from the outside of the peel, then cut them into thin slivers, until you have about a teaspoonful.

Add the orange segments and the slivers of zest, together with the sugar and the rose or orange flower water, to the pan and stir well.

Take off the heat and leave to cool.

Cut the pomegranate into quarters, and separate the seeds from the pith, bending the peel backwards in order to release the seeds.

When the pudding is cool, transfer it to a serving dish and scatter with the chopped nuts and pomegranate seeds. This delicious dessert works well with cream or ice cream on the side.

Black bean brownies

Beans adapt surprisingly well to sweet baking, and here you would be forgiven for not spotting their presence, partly because their colour provides the perfect visual camouflage, and their taste is overshadowed by the chocolate. The addition of puréed beans to the usual ingredients brings a moist richness – comfort without the calories, and all the benefits of added fibre, vitamins and minerals. You can just feel them doing you good.

100 g/7 tablespoons butter or margarine
180 g/1 scant cup golden caster or raw cane sugar
45 g/⅓ cup unsweetened cocoa powder
250 g/1¼ cups cooked, soaked dried black beans, drained
2 eggs
125 g/1 cup self-raising/rising flour
60 g/½ cup roasted hazelnuts, chopped, plus extra to decorate

Serves 6–8

Preheat the oven to 180°C (350°F) Gas 4.

Grease a 28 x 18-cm/11 x 7-in. baking pan and line with baking parchment.

Using a food processor, cream the butter or margarine, sugar, cocoa powder, black beans and eggs together until smooth. Sift the flour into the mixture and fold in gently. Stir in the chopped nuts.

Spoon the batter into the baking pan and bake for about 30 minutes.

Leave to cool in the baking pan for a few minutes, then cut into squares or fingers and turn onto a rack to cool. Sprinkle with extra chopped nuts, to decorate.

Bean torta with walnuts and lemon

In Hungary and other Central European countries, they make a cake not with wheat flour but with cooked beans and maize meal. No fat is added, but it is moist and light, not at all what you might expect, and keeps quite well for several days. I used canned beans to save time, rather than soaking and cooking dried ones, and found they worked perfectly.

75 g/⅔ cup fine maize meal or polenta/cornmeal
350 g/1¾ cups cooked, soaked dried cannellini or haricot/navy beans, or the contents of 1½ x 400-g/14-oz. cans, drained
4 eggs, separated
2 teaspoons pure vanilla extract
275 g/1⅓ cups caster/ granulated sugar, or to taste
grated zest and freshly squeezed juice of 1 lemon
85 g/3 oz. walnuts, finely ground

Serves 8–10

Preheat the oven to 200°C (400°F) Gas 6.

Grease and flour a 23-cm/9-in. round cake pan.

Use a food processor to blend the maize meal or polenta/cornmeal and the beans into a smooth mixture.

Cream the yolks, vanilla extract and 175 g/¾ cup of the sugar together until pale and creamy, then add the mixture to the bean mixture with the grated lemon zest. Blend together thoroughly, then transfer to a large bowl and fold in the ground walnuts.

In a clean bowl, whisk the egg whites until stiff, then carefully fold them into the bean mixture, using a metal spoon. Turn the mixture into the greased and floured cake pan, and bake in the oven for about 30–40 minutes, turning the temperature down to 180°C (350°F) Gas 4 after 20 minutes.

While the cake is cooking, warm the lemon juice with the remaining sugar to make a glaze. When the cake is light brown on top and nicely risen, take it out of the oven and pour the lemon juice and sugar mixture over the surface, then allow to cool in the pan for about 20 minutes. As it cools, the topping will form a crunchy icing.

Suppliers & stockists

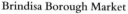

UK

Pulses

Golspie Mill
Dunrobin
Golspie
Sutherland KW10 6SF
Scotland
www.golspiemill.co.uk
01408 633278
*Peasemeal (stoneground roasted
yellow peas)*

Hodmedods
The Studios, London Road
Brampron, Beckles,
Suffolk NR34 8DQ
www.hodmedods.co.uk
01986 467567
*Split and whole dried fava beans and
peas, including Black Badger (carlin)
peas, all grown in Britain. Also roasted
peas and fava beans for snacking and
canned cooked beans*

Ken Bentley Speciality Foods
31 Market Place
Driffield
Yorks YO25 6HR
carlinpeas.tripod.com
01377 257656
Carlin (Black Badger) peas

Brindisa Borough Market
The Floral Hall
Stoney Street,
Borough Market
London SE1 9AF
www.brindisa.com
020 7407 1036
*Beans, chickpeas, lentils and charcuterie
from Spain*

Delicioso
Unit 14, Tower Business Park,
Berinsfield,
Oxon OX10 7LN
www.delicioso.co.uk
01865 340055
*Beans, chickpeas, lentils and charcuterie
from Spain*

The Food Hall
22-24 Turnpike Lane
London N8 0PS
020 8889 2264
*Ethiopian ingredients including spiced
butter and freshly milled flour for
making injera pancakes*

Green Valley
36-37 Upper Berkeley Street
London W1H 5QF
020 7402 7385
*Lebanese ingredients including pulses,
spices, fresh herbs and flatbread*

Persepolis
28-30 Peckham High Street
London SE15 5DT
www.foratasteofpersia.co.uk
020 7639 8007
*Persian ingredients including barberries,
chickpea flour, fava beans and more.*

Isle of Olive
6c Ada Street
London E8 4QU
www.isleofolive.co.uk
020 7241 6493
Greek fava

Maltby & Greek
Arch 17
Apollo Business Park
Lucey Way
Bermondsey
London SE16 4ET
www.maltbyandgreek.com
020 7993 4548
*Santorini fava peas, chickpeas,
gigantes beans*

Piper's Farm
Cullompton
EX15 1SD
www.pipersfarm.com
10392 881380
*Carlin peas, British chickpeas, lentils
and haricot beans; free-range grass-fed
mutton, lamb, pork, chicken, duck,
sausages, cold-smoked bacon, unsmoked
gammon hock*

Oliveology Borough Market
Unit 43 Three Crown Square
8 Southwark Street
London SE1 1TL
www.oliveology.co.uk
020 7018 8858
*Organic Greek gigantes beans,
fava, lentils*

Meat products

Peelham Farm
Foulden, Berwickshire
Scotland TD15 1UG
www.peelham.co.uk
01890 781328
*Organic ham hocks, dry-cured bacon
and a large range of sausages including
Toulouse. Organic Lleyn mutton and
other meat*

Meat Me At Home
Unit 43
London Stone Business Estate
Broughton Road
London SW8 3QR
www.meatmeathome.com
020 7720 4520
*Cold-smoked duck, chicken and
goose breast*

The Ginger Pig
Unit 7W
Cathedral Street
Borough Market
London SE1 9AG
www.thegingerpig.co.uk
0203 869800
*Smoked and unsmoked ham hocks,
bacon and pure meat Toulouse sausages,
from outdoor-reared, rare breed pigs.
Also a full range of good quality meat
and poultry*

Creedy Carver
Merryfield Farm
Upton Hellions
Crediton
EX17 4AF
www.creedycarver.co.uk
10363 772682
Free-range duck, whole or in portions

Seeds

Seeds of Italy
A1 Phoenix Business Centre
Rosslyn Crescent, Harrow
Middlesex HA1 2SP
www.seedsofitaly.com
020 8427 5020
*Seeds for growing nine different varieties
of borlotti beans, plus black-eyed beans,
butterbean fagioli di Spagna and
cannellini beans*

**Garden Organic Heritage
Seed Library**
Ryton Gardens
Wolston Lane, Coventry
Warwickshire CV8 3LG
www.gardenorganic.org.uk
02476 303 317
*Rare and endangered varieties of bean
seeds available for members, including
coco bicolour, birds' egg and carlin peas*

Real Seeds
PO Box 18
Newport, near Fishguard
Pembrokeshire SA65 0AA
www.realseeds.co.uk
01239 821107
*Seeds for growing Czar and Greek
gigantes beans*

Spices

Seasoned Pioneers
Unit 8, Stadium Court
Stadium Road
Plantation Business Park
Bromborough
Wirral CH62 3RP
www.seasonedpioneers.co.uk
0800 068 2348
*Huge range of spices and authentic spice
blends from all over the world*

US

Online/Mail Order Sources

Bob's Red Mill
13521 SE Pheasant Court
Milwaukie, OR 97222
800 349-2173
www.bobsredmill.com
*A big selection of dried beans and lentils.
Chickpea/gram flour too.*

Kalustyan's Spices and Sweets
123 Lexington Avenue
New York, NY 10016
800 352-3451 or 212 685-3451
www.kalustyans.com
*The specialty food store has been a
Manhattan landmark for more than 70
years. Huge selection of international
beans, grains, preserves, spices and more*

Purcell Mountain Farms
393 Firehouse Road
Moyie Springs, ID
208 267-0627
www.purcellmountainfarms.com
*The Idaho company offers more than
100 varieties of dried beans and lentils,
including a large offering of organic beans*

**Rancho Gordo
New World Specialty Food**
1924 Yajome Street
Napa, CA 94559
797 259-1935
www.ranchogordo.com
*Based in Napa Valley where most of
the beans are grown, Rancho Gordos
specializes in heirloom and hard-to-find
bean varieties*

Index

A

apricots (dried): Armenian lentil soup 30
  Noah's pudding 148
Armenian lentil soup 30
aubergines (eggplants): lentil moussaka 113
  Syrian aubergine and chickpea ragout 140
  lamb dhansak 101
avocados: black bean salad 70
  quinoa and butter bean salad 78

B

bacon: cassoulet 90
bananas: shallot and banana bhajis 47
barley: Hungarian red bean hotpot 93
bean torta with walnuts and lemon 152
beans, types of 6–8
beetroot: salad of Puy lentils with roasted beetroot 75
'Beluga' lentils 9
bhajis, shallot and banana 47
bicarbonate of soda/baking soda 16
bicolour beans 7
bird's egg beans 7, 72
black beans: black bean brownies 151
  black bean burgers 60
  black bean salad 70
  Cuban black bean and red pepper soup 38
  Moors and Christians 130
black-eyed beans/peas 10–11
  black-eyed beans and squash in coconut milk 126
  Brazilian black-eyed bean and prawn fritters 49
  cooking times 17
  hoppin' John 105
  salad of marinated chicken and

black-eyed beans 76
black gram (urid beans) 11, 14
  lamb dhansak with squash and lentils 101
black lentil pancakes 46
black turtle beans 6–7
borlotti beans 6, 72, 73
  stew of borlotti beans 121
bottled beans 15
Brazilian black-eyed bean and prawn fritters 49
broad beans (fresh)
  broad bean soup for springtime 37
brown lentils 9
brownies, black bean 151
burgers, black bean 60
butter/lima beans 6, 8, 72
  oven-baked Greek butter beans 110
  Persian pilgrim's soup 115
  quinoa and butter bean salad 78
  succotash 129
buying beans 15–16

C

cakes: bean torta with walnuts and lemon 152
  black bean brownies 151
canned beans 15
cannellini beans 6
  seared squid with white beans and fennel 84
  cassoulet 90
  hot and sour Serbian bean soup 21
  white beans and clams 86
  bean torta with walnuts and lemon 152
  Noah's pudding 148
  Senate bean soup 22
  Valencian paella 83
Caribbean rosecoco beans 7
cassoulet 90
Castelluccio lentils 9
Catalan rice 89
chana dal 11
cheese: Georgian bean pies 56
  lentil moussaka 113

Mrs Harwood's cheese and lentil pie 109
chestnuts: lentil and chestnut soup 33
chicken: chicken kdra 94
  salad of marinated chicken and black-eyed beans 76
  Valencian paella 83
chickpea/gram flour 8
  chickpea fritters 44
  shallot and banana bhajis 47
chickpeas/garbanzos 6, 8, 14
  Catalan rice with chickpeas, smoked haddock and red pepper 89
  chicken kdra 94
  chickpea, egg and potato salad 79
  cooking times 17
  lamb dhansak 101
  Lebanese houmous 138
  Moroccan harira soup 26
  Noah's pudding 148
  Persian lamb casserole 98
  Persian pilgrim's soup 115
  spiced chickpea and spinach pasties 63
  sweet Sicilian pastries 144
  Syrian aubergine and chickpea ragout 140
chicory/endive: purée of fava beans and sautéed chicory 135
  salad of flageolet beans and fennel 68
chillies/chiles: salsa 38, 49
  the simplest dal 136
chocolate: black bean brownies 151
  sweet Sicilian pastries 144
clams, white beans with 86
coconut: moong dal with coconut parippu 127
coconut milk, black-eyed beans and squash in 126
cooking beans 16–17
cooking vessels 28–9
corn cobs: hoppin' John 105
  succotash 129

cottage cheese: sweet fava bean
    tart 147
cranberry beans 7
Cuban black bean and red pepper
    soup 38
cucumber: mint raita 46
    mung bean salad 69

D

dal 11
    the simplest dal 136
dip, Greek fava 139
dosas, Indian lentil and rice 50
dried beans 15
duck: cassoulet 90
    Hungarian red bean hotpot 93

E

eggplants *see* aubergines
eggs: chickpea, egg and potato
    salad 79
endive *see* chicory

F

fagioli di Spagna 8, 15, 72
falafel, fava bean 55
farro: Noah's pudding 148
fasting 118–19
fava beans (split dried) 6, 10, 14
    fava bean falafel 55
    cooking times 17
    Greek fava dip 139
    purée of fava beans and sautéed
        chicory 135
    sweet fava bean tart 147
fava peas (Greek): Greek fava dip
    139
feasts 118–19
fennel: salad of flageolet beans
    and fennel 68
    seared squid with white beans
        and fennel 84
    stew of borlotti beans with
        fennel 121
festivals 58–9, 118–19
fibre 12
flageolet beans 7–8
    salad of flageolet beans and
        fennel 68

sorrel and bean soup 25
flatulence 13
French split pea soup 45
fritters: Brazilian black-eyed bean
    and prawn fritters 49
    chickpea fritters 44

G

garbanzos *see* chickpeas
Georgian bean pies 56
Georgian red bean salad 66
gram flour *see* chickpea flour
Greek fava dip 139
growing beans 72–3
guinea fowl pot-roast 97

H

ham: hoppin' John 105
    Hungarian red bean hotpot 93
    London Particular 40
    salad of flageolet beans and
        fennel 68
    Senate bean soup 22
harira soup, Moroccan 26
health benefits 12–13
heritage varieties 11
hoppin' John 105
hot and sour Serbian bean soup
    21
houmous, Lebanese 138
Hungarian red bean hotpot 93

I

Indian lentil and rice dosas 50
injera pancakes 116

K

kidney beans *see* red kidney
    beans; white kidney beans
Korean moong pancakes with
    pork 52

L

lamb: lamb dhansak 101
    Moroccan harira soup 26
    Persian lamb casserole 98
Lebanese houmous 138
leeks: potage Saint-Germain 34
    sorrel and bean soup 25

legumes 6
lentils 6, 8–9
    Armenian lentil soup 30
    black lentil pancakes 46
    cooking times 17
    Indian lentil and rice dosas 50
    lamb dhansak 101
    lentil and chestnut soup 33
    lentil moussaka 113
    Mrs Harwood's cheese and
        lentil pie 109
    Moroccan harira soup 26
    Persian pilgrim's soup 115
    pot-roast guinea fowl 97
    salad of Puy lentils with roasted
        beetroot 75
    the simplest dal 136
lentils (green, Puy) 9
    lentil and chestnut soup 33
    lentil moussaka 113
    Moroccan harira soup 26
    pot-roast guinea fowl 97

salad of Puy lentils with roasted
beetroot 75
lentils (red) 11
Armenian lentil soup 30
lamb dhansak with squash and
lentils 101
Mrs Harwood's cheese and
lentil pie 109
Persian pilgrim's soup 115
the simplest dal 136
lima beans *see* butter beans
London Particular 40

M

mangoes: mung bean salad 69
maple peas, mutton stew with
102
minerals 12
mint raita 46
Mrs Harwood's cheese and lentil
pie 109
moong dal/mung beans 11, 14
cooking times 17
Korean moong pancakes with
pork 52
moong dal with coconut
parippu 127
mung bean salad 69
Persian pilgrim's soup 115
Moors and Christians 130
Moroccan harira soup 26
moussaka, lentil 113
munazalit bathinjan 140
mung beans *see* moong dal
mushrooms: black bean burgers
60
red beans à la bourguignonne
122
mutton stew 102

N

Noah's pudding 148
noodles: Persian pilgrim's soup
115

O

oranges: Noah's pudding 148
oven-baked Greek butter beans
110

P

paella, Valencian 83
pancakes: black lentil pancakes
46
Indian lentil and rice dosas 50
injera pancakes 116
Korean moong pancakes with
pork 52
parsley oil 84
parsnips: hot and sour Serbian
bean soup 21
pasties, spiced chickpea and
spinach 63
pastries, sweet Sicilian 144
pastry 63
saffron pastry 147
peas (dried green & yellow split)
6, 9–10
Greek fava dip 139
London Particular 40
potage Saint-Germain 34
split pea stew with Ethiopian
spices 116
peas (fresh): potage Saint-
Germain 34
peppers: Armenian lentil soup 30
Catalan rice 89
Cuban black bean and red
pepper soup 38
hoppin' John 105
Moors and Christians 130
Persian lamb casserole 98

Persian pilgrim's soup 115
Phaseolus beans 6–8
pies: Georgian bean pies 56
spiced chickpea and spinach
pasties 63
sweet Sicilian pastries 144
pigeon peas/toor dal: lamb
dhansak 101
pinto beans 7
refried beans 132
Le Poiré-sur-Vie 58
pomegranates: Georgian red
bean salad 66
pork: cassoulet 90
Korean moong pancakes with
pork 52
potage Saint-Germain 34
potatoes: chickpea, egg and
potato salad 79
Senate bean soup 22
shallot and banana bhajis 47
prawns: Brazilian black-eyed
bean and prawn fritters 49
pressure cookers 17
protein 12–13
pulses 6

Q

quinoa and butter bean salad 78

R

raisins: Noah's pudding 148
raita, mint 46
red kidney beans 7, 13–14
  Georgian bean pies 56
  Georgian red bean salad 66
  Hungarian red bean hotpot 93
  Persian pilgrim's soup 115
  red beans à la bourguignonne 122
refried beans 132
rice: Catalan rice with chickpeas, smoked haddock and red pepper 89
  hoppin' John 105
  Indian lentil and rice dosas 50
  Moors and Christians 130
  Noah's pudding 148
  Valencian paella 83
runner beans 8, 72
  Valencian paella 83

S

saffron: saffron pastry 147
  white beans with clams 86
salads: black bean salad 70
  chickpea, egg and potato salad 79
  flageolet beans and fennel 68
  Georgian red bean salad 66
  marinated chicken and black-eyed beans 76
  mung bean salad 69
  Puy lentils with roasted beetroot 75
  quinoa and butter bean salad 78
salsa 38, 49
Santa Pau 58
sauce, tahini 55
sausages: cassoulet 90
  Hungarian red bean hotpot 93
scritto beans 7
Senate bean soup 22
Serbian bean soup 21
shallot and banana bhajis 47
shrimp see prawns
the simplest dal 136
slow cookers 17

smoked haddock: Catalan rice 89
soaking beans 16
sofrito 38
sorrel and bean soup 25
soups: Armenian lentil soup 30
  broad bean soup for springtime 37
  Cuban black bean and red pepper soup 38
  hot and sour Serbian bean soup 21
  lentil and chestnut soup 33
  London Particular 40
  Moroccan harira soup 26
  Persian pilgrim's soup 115
  potage Saint-Germain 34
  Senate bean soup 22
  sorrel and bean soup 25
soya beans/soybeans 11, 14
spinach: Persian pilgrim's soup 115
  spiced chickpea and spinach pasties 63
  split pea stew with Ethiopian spices 116
split peas see peas (dried green & yellow split)
squash: black-eyed beans and squash in coconut milk 126
  lamb dhansak with squash and lentils 101
  succotash 129
squid: seared squid with white beans and fennel 84
stews: cassoulet 90
  chicken kdra 94
  mutton stew 102
  Persian lamb casserole 98
  split pea stew with Ethiopian spices 116
  stew of borlotti beans with fennel 121
  Syrian aubergine and chickpea ragout 140
storing beans 15–16
succotash 129
sultanas: Noah's pudding 148
Syrian aubergine and chickpea ragout 140

T

tahini: Lebanese houmous 138
  spiced chickpea and spinach pasties 63
  tahini sauce 55
Tarbais beans 72
tarka 136
tart, sweet fava bean 147
tomatoes: lentil moussaka 113
  oven-baked Greek butter beans 110
  salsa 38, 49
  stew of borlotti beans with fennel 121
Tongue of Fire beans 7
toor dal see pigeon peas
toxins 13–14, 73
traditional cooking vessels 28–9

U

urid beans see black gram
urid dal: Indian lentil and rice dosas 50

V

Valencian paella 83
vinaigrette 68, 78
vitamins 12

W

walnuts: bean torta with walnuts and lemon 152
  Georgian red bean salad 66
water, soaking beans 16
white beans 8, 14
  cassoulet 90
  hot and sour Serbian bean soup 21
  Noah's pudding 148
  seared squid with white beans and fennel 84
  white beans with clams 86
  see also cannellini beans
white kidney beans 14

Y

yogurt: lentil moussaka 113
  mint raita 46

Acknowledgements

Grateful thanks are due to my husband Grant Muter, for his constant support and for cheerfully eating his way through innumerable leguminous meals without complaint. His company on our many journeys of discovery in the world of beans was also much appreciated. Also thanks to all of my friends, family and neighbours who have taken part in the beanfeasts in our kitchen and offered their invaluable comments.

My gratitude also to Stephen Anderton, Lynda Bransbury, Peter and Rebecca Child, Michael Fleischer, Arshida Hindocha, Peter Lapinskas, Mehri Madadi, Katie Rock, Afreen Saville, Alice Wooledge Salmon, Edith Struthers, Subin Subhash, Chris Wardle and Annie Wright, for their perceptive advice on culinary and other matters.

Also to Andrew Jacobs, Managing Director of importers and distributors Poortman UK, for introducing me to pulses on a global scale.

Thanks also to the team at Ryland Peters & Small, especially my editor Nathan Joyce for seeing the whole project through from beginning to end with such dedication, efficiency and enthusiasm. Also to Julia Charles, Leslie Harrington, Barbara Zúñiga, Rosie Reynolds, Linda Berlin and William Reavell, who all deserve special thanks for their valuable contributions.

Amongst the many books that I have used for reference, the following have been especially useful. *The Oxford Companion to Food* by Alan Davidson; *The Oxford Book of Food Plants* by J. G. Vaughan and C. A. Geissler; *Beans, A History,* by Ken Albala; *On Food and Cooking* by Harold McGee; and *The Frugal Gourmet on our Immigrant Ancestors* by Jeff Smith.